— YES —

THE ARABS CAN TOO

‑ YES ‑

THE ARABS CAN TOO

Mohamed Bin Issa Al Jaber

Special Envoy of the Director General of UNESCO
for Tolerance, Democracy and Peace

Foreword by
Professor Michael Worton
Vice-Provost, University College London (UCL)

Arabian Publishing

Yes, The Arabs Can Too
By Mohamed Bin Issa Al Jaber

© Mohamed Bin Issa Al Jaber 2013

Produced and published in 2013 by Arabian Publishing Ltd
4 Bloomsbury Place, London WC2A 2QA
Email: arabian.publishing@arabia.uk.com
www.oxbowbooks.com/oxbow/arabianpublishing

Translated and edited by Philip Gordon and William Facey
from the first Arabic edition *Na'm ... al-'Arab aydan qādirūn*.
Beirut: Al-Dār al-Maṣriyyah al-Lubnāniyyah, 2009

A catalogue card for this book is available from the British Library

ISBN: 978-0-9571060-9-3

Typesetting and digital artwork by Jamie Crocker, Artista-Design, UK
Printed and bound by TJ International, Cornwall, UK

There is enough in the world for everybody's need,
but not enough for everybody's greed

Mahatma Gandhi

CONTENTS

FOREWORD

O<small>UR COMPLEX AND RAPIDLY</small> changing 21st century is perhaps best defined by the phenomenon of globalisation. However, as we think and speak increasingly about the 'global village', recognising the ubiquity of strong brands of consumer goods and the ever greater dominance of English as the lingua franca of international interactions, we need to acknowledge and address the attendant paradox that cultural differences are becoming more pronounced and more important, yet less and less understood.

Globalisation is also changing the ways in which the world's economies are run, with international economic organisations ranging from the G20 to the IMF to the major financial services companies, as well as the massive multi-national companies and corporations, exercising ever-growing power. Furthermore, we now have to cope with the fact that the world economy is witnessing a significant shift in the balance of economic and financial power away from the West towards the East.

Across the world, we see growing demands for reforms in political systems, whether this be in the 'Arab Spring', or in the shift to the right in many countries across Europe, or the growing demands for democratisation in the Far East. And the new social media technologies are fostering the emergence of local, then national and often ultimately international protest movements against social and economic inequalities, such as the Occupy Movement and the Make Poverty History campaign.

This complexity means that we have to learn to think simultaneously both in terms of the global and international and the local and national, recognising that there are new interplays at work between them, as significant re-balancings of power assert themselves in the world.

We therefore need guidance – and we need to be encouraged, and sometimes even shocked out of our traditional mind-sets. Sheikh Mohamed Bin Issa Al Jaber is well placed to do this, having already established himself internationally as a major social, cultural and political commentator.

He has achieved breath-taking success as a businessman through his uncanny feel for market trends. Time and again, he has proved himself to be a master of the unexpected and a clear and lucid forecaster of what only he perceives to be the inevitable. At one point, for example, he predicted the dangers of the overheating of the world economy and warned against what he called the 'illusion of wealth'. This is just one example of his insights. There are many more, and what marks all of his interventions is his moral courage. He is outspoken in his advocacy of transparency, of good governance and of appropriate and rigorous governments, just as he is fearless in his criticisms of both Western and Arab regimes when they have fallen short of these ideals.

Characteristic of his business acumen is his ability to cross frontiers between different countries, continents and cultures. This ability to move across demarcation lines, to make links, to think 'outside the box', has given him a marvellous openness of spirit and an ability to respond to the people he meets. It was thus in many ways inevitable (and appropriate) that he should direct his vision and much of his activity to working with and speaking on behalf of international organisations, such as the UN and UNESCO, for whom he is a Special Envoy of the Director General for Tolerance, Democracy and Peace.

This book is a translation of the Arabic original, which was first written and published in 2009. It therefore pre-dates the events of the 'Arab Spring' and other recent upheavals in the Arab world. Its insights are none the less valid, and are just as applicable to the Arab world today as they were four years ago. Indeed, they have taken on an extra urgency in the light of the author's prescient diagnosis of the Arab peoples' thirst for democracy, freedom, human rights and proper citizenship in their own countries. In it, he speaks as a true and committed Arab, whilst also speaking as a global citizen, addressing both his fellow Arabs and individuals, business organisations and governments throughout the world.

He analyses, anatomises and challenges failing and out-dated systems; it is also a call to action, urging us all to engage in the process of creating a more equitable future for all. Speaking with both pride and lucidity about Arab history, tradition and culture, he argues that Arabs have become 'strangers in their country', largely because they have become complicit in consumerism without thinking enough about the need for home-grown productivity and social and economic growth.

The book is informed by a profound belief in the essential creativity of Arabs and their innate ability to reform, modernise and liberalise whilst remaining faithful to the essence of Arab and Islamic culture. Sheikh Mohamed is very proud of Arab culture, and he is greatly distressed by the fact that so much of the information about the Arab mentality that reaches the West nowadays is negative and even hate-filled. In fact, as he once commented ruefully, 'the information revolution has not yet led to a revolution in understanding'.

It is an all too regrettable fact of our world that it seems unable to exist without narratives of conflict, and part of Sheikh Mohamed's mission is to inflect such narratives in the direction of mutual under-standing and enrichment, in a delight in plurality and in a commitment to open government and good governance.

He courageously questions whether the notion of the state itself is the biggest loser in the globalisation process – in which the market seems to reign supreme. Furthermore, whilst acutely aware of the necessity of sustainable development, he provocatively but justifiably argues that it has become such a fashionable and dominant concept that it risks evacuating the fundamental concept of the public interest and public service.

On page after page of this book, he uncovers and analyses the complexities and paradoxes which inform the new world order. This work is intended as an encouragement to Arabs to reform their political and economic processes, whilst remaining true to the values that through the centuries have underpinned the best of Arab beliefs and endeavours. Sheikh Mohamed does not preach, though: he offers messages of how this process must be one of integration with the rest of the world whilst also retaining Arab integrity and specificity.

However, this publication is much more than a book on and for the Arab world. It offers advice and detailed, practical ways forward not only for Arabs, but also for peoples throughout the world, as we all struggle to comprehend and respond creatively to globalisation and the seismic socio-economic and political shifts which it is bringing about.

Sheikh Mohamed teaches us all many lessons in this book, though never in a patronising way. He writes in a spirit of sharing and encouraging. The challenge for us readers is first of all to read him properly and attentively and then, crucially, to act on his advice.

Professor Michael Worton
Vice-Provost, University College London (UCL)
May 2013

— YES —

THE ARABS CAN TOO

Introduction

THE STATE OF THE WORLD at the end of the 21st century's first decade can be summed up by just a handful of events. The most salient are the end of the Cold War and collapse of the Eastern Bloc followed by the Soviet Union's disintegration, the progressive unification of much of Europe, the spectacular rise of China and India, eclipsing Japan's, and the catastrophe of 9/11 with the re-orientation of the United States' global strategy consequent upon it.

These developments have been accompanied by a profound change, the move to a post-industrial era, even as the process of transforming the world into a global village accelerates – a process that is perhaps also the result of that change. The new age of communications technology, digital information and the knowledge-based society will engender a new framework of economic, social and political relations.

At a time when the rest of the world is making the transition to a post-industrial society, the Arab world is still tentatively trying to enter its industrial age – a phase that elsewhere has been consigned to the past. Despite these efforts, the Arab world remains above all an economic zone of consumption. It wears what it does not weave. It eats what it does not grow. And to a large extent it uses what it does not manufacture.

Although Arab societies all conform rather obviously to this model, they conceal at the same time an extremely complex variation and diversity. Nonetheless the general view of these societies from the outside is of remnants from a bygone age, survivals of traditional passivity inherited from a time of religious and colonial domination. Outsiders see among the Arabs only feudal systems and paternalistic societies, the servitude of women, a hatred of freedom, and pervasive corruption and tyranny. The outside world, looking in through its antique lens, fails to discern the dynamic changes propelling various sectors of Arab society forward, and inspiring a quantum leap in the attempt to catch up with international progress, as a new generation of Arabs presses for advancement, improvement in living conditions and the shaking off of the shackles of tyranny.

So it is with Arab societies in general. The individual Arab citizen, on the other hand, feels himself to be an alien within his own country, a negativity accentuated whenever he compares his own subject condition at home with that of citizens of non-Arab countries. Thus he observes European or American citizens behaving as if their countries actually belonged to them, taking for granted their right to influence their development and improvement. By contrast, Arabs in general feel themselves to be strangers in their own home – a feeling of estrangement that intensifies with poverty and ignorance, even while their lands contain much of the world's mineral wealth and, in the past, have made a great contribution to world civilisation and intellectual history.

Awareness cannot be generated from outside the time and circumstances of an individual's life. If Arab citizens are to replace the negative feelings they currently suffer with a positive sense of being free citizens empowered to exert some control over their lives and societies, they must first of all be liberated from the culture of conspiracy, predestination and ancestral ideology into which they have been born, and acknowledge and respect the experiences of other peoples. Of course their starting point must be their own society with its own material conditions and level of progress, but they then also have to become productive citizens in an evolving society. They must cease to be prisoners of the past – a legacy that their rigid imagination has elevated into an unchanging, ideal world disconnected from the reality of the passing of ages.

As Arabs we have to face up to the law of history that ordains that the flame of civilisation passes from one culture that has become set in its ways, to another that seeks to modernize and develop, with new ideas and new inventions opening up the prospect of a changed modernity. We also have to realise that any innovation, just as in the past, will encounter resistance from entrenched attitudes that cling to tradition, reject all change and modernization, and recoil from joining the onward march of progress, and will face opposition from dictators intent on maintaining the status quo and establishing dynasties.

If we genuinely wish to improve our living conditions ourselves, and catch up with progress elsewhere, the first vital step on that path is to re-evaluate the function and role of the state and its moral duties towards its own citizens. We must promote the public interest above every other consideration, and take action to provide those able to work with the basic necessities of good health and a good education, equipping them to meet the needs of society and the economy in a country under the rule of law.

Proper rule of law entails all government decisions being taken within the framework of the constitution and in strict accordance with statute. Laws must be binding on all citizens without exception and must be enforced without discrimination on the basis of social status, function, gender, religion or ethnic origin. They must be applied by an even-handed judiciary that is independent, professional, transparent and rigorous. The courts must issue their rulings impartially in accordance with legality and justice. Without a transparent legal framework and a just administrative and legal system a society can never achieve real growth: it is impossible to provide incentives for the private sector to invest if there are no clear laws regulating commerce, customs, agreements and contracts, the protection of private property and individual rights. These laws must be universally respected and implemented with integrity and transparency. Obscurity, complexity and contradiction in laws and regulations, or in their interpretation or implementation, are the enemy of private investment in the official economy, and encourage the black market and other unofficial business activity. Corruption, fraud and nepotism flourish, stifling honest competition. Ultimately it is the poor who suffer most from the unofficial market economy, and such conditions pose an impediment to successful and sustainable growth, investment and development.

From this follows the need for clarity and simplification in drawing up regulations to control investment activity, credit and deposits, taxation, and the establishment and liquidation of businesses. Transparent employment laws must protect workers from exploitation and guarantee the employment of women. Mechanisms must be put in place for participation in the workplace, for the protection of the poor and to guarantee food security.

Sustainable growth requires a primary role for a national investment programme based on savings, with the important safeguard that existing financial institutions demonstrate their ability effectively to allocate capital funds to productive investments. Direct foreign investment undoubtedly plays an important role in stimulating growth, but it must be complementary to local investments, not an alternative to them.

These days investment in human resources has become a fundamental precondition for economic growth, development and production. Today's world is remarkable for the sheer speed of technological innovation and its rapid transformation into knowledge-based societies. As a result workers' skills now require continual renewal to enable them to keep up with technology and digital innovation. Investment in continuous education and training is today the true seed capital of production and wealth, and a necessary condition of being able to carry out proper public services and functions. In the public sphere, a firmly rooted institutional culture is essential, in which employees act in the service both of the organisation itself and of the state and the public interest. The institution should not exist to serve its staff. If governments wish firmly to establish proper institutional culture, the principle of impartial, objective and transparent selection of employees must be paramount, such that special pleading, nepotism and undue influence are eliminated.

Governments must put in place systems preventing conflicts of interest, and mechanisms of accountability, monitoring and transparency to ensure impartial bidding processes and to combat corruption, fraud and bribery. Workers must be encouraged by rewards for moral integrity, professionalism and conscientious performance. We shall deal with all these things in more depth in the following chapters. First we shall take the long historical view by way of defining the concept of globalisation. We shall also deal in detail with the importance of collaboration between the public and private sectors, and with the reforms and modernisation undertaken by various Western countries as they seek to develop new and creative approaches to the challenges of globalisation, the environment and sustainable growth. A sound approach to sustainable growth combines respect for the environment and social justice with the pursuit of economic and financial gain. Sustainable growth adds new economic, social and environmental value.

Achieving such goals will require a gradual merger of the unofficial with the official economy through legal and regulatory reform and the enhanced role of the rule of law. Shared consultative mechanisms will have to bridge the public and private sectors. Workers' representatives, trade unions, and also business owners and representatives from the informal economy must be included in this process, so that they can all work together to achieve the creation of a fully functioning official economy.

Collaboration of this kind between the public and private sectors will require the expertise of bodies in civil society, and also monitoring by them. Such monitoring should extend to co-operation in education and training, particularly with occupational training institutes and schools of business administration, with the aim of improving skills and training experts and leaders for the public and private sectors. The private sector is brimming with massive latent potential in the form of expertise, knowledge and networks, as well as creative talent for finding new ways of achieving sustainable growth. Co-operation between the public and private sectors is thus highly desirable, but success will also depend on engaging all stake-holders – workers, trade unions and civil society – in management and constructive criticism of the collaborative programmes, if sustainable growth is to be achieved.

In today's world the state bears a massive responsibility for managing the process of integrating with the global economy on the one hand, while achieving national economic and social objectives on the other, as we shall see later on. Among the basic functions of the state are the provision of universal education and health care, safeguarding social welfare, maintaining the sovereignty of the law, and investment in the physical and social infrastructure. The state also plays an important role in limiting the impact of globalisation on low-income groups through progressive taxation and social programmes. Banding together with other countries to form a large market is one correct and effective means of ensuring social security and stability. An aggressive approach to economic competition and investment in research and development, have also to be maintained. Globalisation has without doubt arisen and flourished in an ethical vacuum, in which the success or failure of the market has been the sole criterion for behaviour, according to the principle that 'the winner takes all'. This situation has led to an understandable demand for a more ethical globalisation.

As barriers of time and space have shrunk thanks to the rise and spread of modern technology, and in particular of telecommunications, it is information technology that has created the conditions for globalisation to forge ahead. The cost of communications has fallen, whether of moving information between people, or of moving goods and capital across continents. This has led to the expansion of direct foreign investment and the phenomenon of capital flows across borders. Ever-increasing competition in international markets has compelled countries to lower national barriers to international business, seeking to attract it and give it space to operate.

Modern technology has put knowledge at the forefront of production, and today high-tech industries are the fastest-growing sectors in economic development. What is needed is a renewed affirmation of the strategic value of investment in education and training of the widest scope, and in the creation of knowledge-based societies.

The following chapters set out to deal with these objectives in depth and detail, and my hope is that the reader will enjoy exploring them. They are of course no more than a personal effort, but I hope they can be of some benefit as we Arabs set off along the path of reform and change in pursuit of modernisation, and as we promote Arab participation in creating the civilisation of the 21st century.

God is behind the intention.

Mohamed Bin Issa Al Jaber

1

The Arabs Past and Present

FOR SIX WHOLE CENTURIES Arab civilisation was cosmopolitan in
outlook, and open to all peoples and influences. Ideas and inventions
were adopted from the ancient world and remoulded in the furnace of
Islam to take their place at the heart of a culture that found unity in
variety. The Arabic language became the vehicle for new ideas in
jurisprudence, the Hadith (Prophetic tradition) and the interpretation
of the Qur'an, along with grammar, literary expression, poetry, philosophy, Sufi mysticism, astronomy, mathematics, and the empirical and
experimental sciences including chemistry, physics and the study of the
natural world. Arabs and other Muslims created an advanced civilisation
with an assured place in the history of human progress, and Islam as a
dominant religion and culture absorbed invaders and barbarians, who
converted to it. Though Muslims had to suffer the rule of outsiders for
short periods, for example during the Mongol invasions and the
Crusades, the Mongols became Muslims, and the Crusaders were
eventually expelled.

At its pinnacle between the 8th and 11th centuries AD, Islamic civilisation depended on the genius and inventiveness primarily of the Arabs, with the Persians coming a close second. Later centuries brought the contribution of the Turks to the forefront, with their distinctive military and expansionist ethos, while the Arabs and Persians devoted themselves to cultural, political and scientific pursuits.

Between the 16th and 19th centuries Muslims were divided into three imperial spheres – the Ottoman state, Safavid and Qajar Persia, and the Mughal realm in India. The Ottomans and Mughals were concerned less with science and culture than with military technology and engineering. The contrary was the case in Persia, where an intellectual revival led by major thinkers took place. However this Shi'ite school of thought drew its strength from tradition rather than reformism. In this atmosphere judicial initiative (*ijtihad*) became the source of tradition: the enlightened innovators were regarded as the repositories of authority on tradition and the primary sources, giving rise to two schools of thought, the Usuliyya as against the Ikhbariyya. Essentially the Usuliyya tendency allowed deduction by comparison and analogy – *qiyas* – in the formulation of legal opinions and rulings, whereas the Ikhbariyya relied exclusively on the original sources of the Qur'an and Hadith.

Meanwhile various reform movements and religious schools sprang up within Islamic societies, the most potent of which was undoubtedly the Wahhabi movement initiated by Muhammad bin 'Abd al-Wahhab (1703–92), the powerful and original 18th-century religious reformer in central Arabia. His call preceded all other reform movements in modern Islam and influenced them. Furthermore, his message was the only one not influenced by the outside world. It had an internal dynamic for Islam. Wahhabism breathes fresh life into the Hanbali teaching that insists on the unitary nature and sanctity of God Almighty. It eradicated the veneration of saints, even of the Companions and family of the Prophet, and rejected the Sufi mystical movement. Ibn Hanbal (AD 780–855) was himself also famous for his resistance to the rationalist Mu'tazilite thinkers, and the Hanbali School was well known for its opposition to the Shi'ites.

The Wahhabi movement was contemporary with the 18th-century

European Enlightenment, that culturally and philosophically important phenomenon emerging originally in France, Germany and Britain during a half-century or so between 1720 and 1770. Enlightenment thinkers were characterised by their opposition to both religion and absolute rule, and by their promotion of the unlimited power of the intellect.

Enlightenment philosophy called for a break with European Christianity and its past. In contrast, many Muslim thinkers representing the revival never thought of the phenomena of enlightenment and modernity as necessitating a break with their cultural inheritance. Rather the contrary. They sought to accommodate tradition, and did not regard rational enlightenment as a means of liberation from a stultifying past.

Thus the Arab revival began as a linguistic and literary movement arising from contact with Europe, rather than as a movement for social or religious reform. Among its most significant figures were Butrus Al-Bustani (1819–83), Naseef Ibrahim Al-Yaziji (1800–71), Mahmoud Sami Al-Baroudi (1838–1904), Adeeb Ishaq (1856–85) and Ibrahim Al-Muwailihi (1846–1906). They achieved distinction for their dictionaries, poetry and literature. They were reformers of the Arabic language and pioneers of literary style, and set about rediscovering the past in order to express the present. They wrested Arabic from the religious scholars and put it to secular and modernising uses.

The most prominent of those who did draw inspiration from the ideas of philosophical enlightenment accompanying the new surge of scientific discovery, the emergence of the nation state and the drive to religious reform were Rifa'ah Al-Tahtawi (1801–73), 'Abd al-Rahman Al-Kawakibi (1849–1902), Khair al-Din Al-Tunisi (1822–90), Farah Antun (1874–1922) and Qasim Ameen (1863–1908). The revival's flourishing in Egypt owed much to Jamal al-Din Al-Afghani (1838–97), Muhammad 'Abduh (1849–1905) and Rashid Rida (1865–1935) during the reign of the Khedive Ismail (1863–79), and Egypt became its centre, embracing the outpouring of cultural Arabism just as it welcomed the trend towards religious reform.

The objective of these scholars and thinkers was cultural revival and religious, political and social reform as seen from the perspective of an intellectual, secular modernisation. There is no doubt that Presidents Mustapha Kamal in Turkey, Bourguiba in Tunisia and Nasser in Egypt were influenced by this reforming outlook, that also produced cultural luminaries such as Mohamed Hassanein Heikal (b. 1923), Ali 'Abd al-Razzaq (1888–1966), Ahmed Lutfi Al-Sayed (1872–1963), Salama Mousa (1887–1958), Taha Hussein (1889–1973) and many others. Then came the '60s and '70s of the last century and Islam was marginalised in political debate. Some chose to glorify Marxism and nationalist revolution. Others trumpeted the American ideology of change. This went on until the 1979 Iranian upheaval, which rekindled the traditional concept of revolution and extinguished the equation of progress with liberation from religion. The motive force behind Ayatollah Khomeini's revolution was an explicit return to traditional Islam.

One can discern in the Arab world today two conflicting ideological trends. The first calls for modernity and places emphasis on such issues as innovation and progress, Arabism and Islam, democracy and freedom, cultural revival and Westernisation. Even though this trend promotes freedom of critical thought, it still produces little in the way of originality.

The second trend, under the slogan of restoring Islam to society, seeks in effect to transform religion into a mere cultural identity by calling for the application of Shari'a law. In this way the Holy Qur'an is reduced in practical terms merely to its penal system. By thus omitting faith, ethics and theology, this school of thought aims to engage people in political action by promoting religion as no more than a cultural and political banner, and it glorifies the idea of *jihad* as constructed by jurists in response to the circumstances of times long past. However such ideas are in conflict with the values of the modern age that espouse intellectual and political freedom, human dignity and the rights of women. The objective of this second trend is both to purge society of modernising systems and to restore the Islamisation of society.

However this trend, that explicitly rejects the first, is also confronted by a moderate Islamic trend that energises the deeper aspects of Islam and calls for self-reform, openness to others and dialogue with them within the framework of a debate about religion and civilisation. This middle and moderate tendency aims at peaceful coexistence, co-operation and good neighbourliness among religions and peoples.

There is no doubt that successive rule by Mongols, Tartars and Turks over the Islamic world seriously undermined Arab Muslim culture and civilisation, afflicting as it did the great Arab capitals of Damascus, Baghdad and Cairo and even the Arab Maghrib. This Arab submission was followed by a deep political quietism, a lethargy that allowed tribal values and tribal and regional strife to rear their heads again, with each country turning inwards upon itself and failing to keep pace with the transformations taking place in Europe from the 16th century onwards.

It is true that the Ottoman Empire paid homage to the teachings of the Qur'an and adopted the Arabic script and Islamic festivals. Furthermore, from the 16th century the Sultan became the Muslim Caliph. However this severed the caliphate from its Arab origin, the fountainhead of Islamic Arab solidarity. The Ottomans, famed for their warlike proclivities, breathed new life into the jihadist ethos. Their authority was not Arab, and they had a ritualistic approach to belief.

Their educated class was noted for its achievements in architecture, engineering and medicine, and paid no special attention to the Arab Islamic heritage and the Arabic language. It had been very different in an earlier era, in the time of Al-Bukhari (AD 810–70), Al-Tirmidhi (d. *ca*. AD 890), Al-Nisa'i (d. AD 915) and Al-Tabari (AD *ca*. 839–923). Most of these scholars were of Iranian origin but their language was Arabic and they specialised in the Prophetic traditions, the interpretation of the Qur'an and Islamic historiography. They were well versed in Arab traditions and genealogy, and they loved Arab Islamic culture – in fact they adopted it as their own, and developed it. There is little comparison between the Islamic cultural instincts of scholars such as these and those of a Turkish scholar in the 16th or 17th century, because the Turkish elite had no allegiance to Arab culture. There existed a complete flourishing cultural world with which Ottomans scholars were unfamiliar, however versed they might be in the Arabic language.

Religious, philosophical and intellectual stagnation took hold from the start of the 17th century as the Ottoman caliphate closed all doors to initiative. Although Al-Azhar University, the Zaitouna Mosque and Qairawan preserved their ancient heritage, intellectual inertia was accompanied by rigidity in jurisprudence. The obstacles to judicial initiative heralded the end for nineteen schools of jurisprudence that had helped Islam adapt to the forward march of Arab civilisation and had contributed to a climate in which culture could thrive and evolve. The breakup of the Ottoman Empire as a result of the First World War would create freedom for bolder legal opinions (*fatwas*), but these were unable to match the scholarly, religious and philosophical level of the early schools of Islamic law.

Colonialism, both Ottoman and European, was the spur for the Arab awakening and during the 20th century the Arabs demonstrated an ability to confront it. They were all able to shake off colonial rule – with the exception of Palestine, which has now become a matter of international concern. Circumstances still do not favour an international resolution of this problem despite the massive sacrifices of the Palestinians and their insistence on liberation and independence as they continue to struggle for their existence. One can only hope that the re-election of Barack Obama as President of the United States may redirect Western policy towards a permanent resolution of the Arab–Israeli conflict and the Palestinian issue.

It is certainly true today that the Arab world has begun slowly to reduce the vast gulf separating it from the West. But despite great advances in the spread of education, in medicine, construction, and manufacturing, in the modernisation of agriculture, and in keeping abreast of developments in telecommunications and the media, it still languishes far below the economic, scientific, cultural, technological and military level of the Western world. The Arabs still face the uphill task of nurturing home-grown technical and digital talent, scientific innovation and a productive and revitalised economy.

It is true too that while the Arabs are the beneficiaries of a great linguistic, religious and cultural inheritance, they are currently making no contribution to the evolution of modern culture. Muslim countries today are no longer at the cutting edge of civilisation, as was the case in the Middle Ages when Islam led the world in science, technology and scholarship. That culture, combining the religious with the secular, had lost its dynamism by the end of the 15th century AD.

Nevertheless if we take a general look at Arab creativity today, we can see that it is evenly spread through all Arab countries. It comprises much more than just sporadic successes by lone individuals, in particular some outside the Arab world, in the range of creative modern forms available such as cinema, literature, music, the theatre and the arts, let alone philosophy, history, science, technology, information technology, and even space travel. Yet this output fails to make any real, original impact on the modern world, because Arab cultures in general remain stuck in imitative mode: their gaze is on a civilisation rooted in the past, and they long for the separate identity, language, religious affiliation and pride in tradition that it confers, in order to screen off Muslim Arab civilisation from culture in the rest of the world.

What is needed today is for the intellectual, scientific, technical and literary progress of the West to be studied and digested. Then an Arab strategy for culture and intellectual values should be put in place in the academic and technical arenas, as is happening in China, India and Brazil. A new Arab awareness of the world gives grounds for optimism, as do the strong ties between regions and peoples, the growing openness towards external trends, and the move towards collaboration through the formation of regional organisations determined by common borders, geography and economic interests. This movement will assist in overcoming divisions, and will strengthen the various infrastructures. The economy will take precedence over politics. The role of the state today is that it should enable and facilitate, by providing incentives for material and non-material advancement and by opening up space for civil society to play its part.

The dirigiste state in the Arab world has not moved on from the '60s and '70s of the last century. During the period of revolutions and independence these states were heavily preoccupied by their aims and ambitions. Their leaders were carried away by feelings that they possessed an absolute truth, and showed zero tolerance towards dissenters. This messianic tunnel vision caused every revolution to end in suppression and clamp-downs on democracy, and engendered paranoia, a sense of being persecuted from within and without. This was particularly the case under so-called Communist regimes, and crises were fabricated around which the public could coalesce in a unified emotional reaction. Following independence, all talk was of the need for revolution rather than of reform. The assertion of the revolutionary self, the intoxication of renewal and a desire for constant change leave no scope for objective, realistic planning or for the formulation of long-term strategies for growth and modernisation.

The result of these unrealistic policies with their exaggerated objectives has been that the state today in most Arab countries, especially previously revolutionary ones, is unable to fulfil its original manifesto. Those inflated aims have now been abandoned, resulting in a gradual alienation between the state and the citizen, such that people have begun to live on the margin of the state. Islamic movements have exploited this and begun to occupy the space between the state and the people, and have exploited public anxiety about the future and the sinister aims of more powerful countries. This is done sometimes in the name of economics, and at other times in the name of the ideology of human rights.

In some countries democracy is looked upon merely as a mechanism and its external features have been adopted, such as a variety of political parties, a parliament, elections and the rule of the majority. But they have not adopted its essential spirit, which is the supreme value of the individual, and hence human dignity, human rights and freedom of conscience as the fundamental values of every democracy.

One foundation of democracy is a system of precise checks and balances between social classes and their interests. This militates against hysterical attachment to a dominant ideology, and prevents the machinery of oppression being established by an elite, as was the norm under Communism, in the dictatorships of the Third World, and in various other authoritarian regimes basing their legitimacy on the need to confront alleged problems of identity, heritage, ethnicity, modernity, or political Islam. In truth such regimes are incapable of expressing the real issues in society, and this renders them fragile and exposed to foreign intervention, as has occurred in more than one Arab country. The real issues undermining prospects for growth in the Arab region are fundamentally social, economic and cultural ones. It is poverty, deteriorating housing and the inadequacy of health and social welfare provision that constitute serious obstacles to growth in the Arab world in general.

According to assessments by the World Bank and United Nations Development Programme, poverty is on the rise in terms of both population numbers and income, especially in average-income countries in both East and West. This yawning gap and the imbalance it represents in the distribution of wealth is becoming an increasingly pressing issue.

Also among the most critical problems for Arab countries are the ongoing rise in youth unemployment and the integration of women into Arab labour markets. Success on these two fronts is absolutely vital for ensuring growth and reducing poverty.

The issue of general unemployment too has become a national preoccupation in the countries of the Gulf Co-operation Council. Domination of the economy by the petroleum and energy sector, which requires only a small workforce, and the issue of foreign workers, who outnumber the national workforce, have created huge difficulties for nationals trying to find work, not to mention the related issues of mistreatment of immigrant workers, violations of human rights and the absence of such values among employers. At a regional level the problem of unemployment is linked to the quality of education, and to the mismatch between the skills of graduates and the needs of the labour market.

It is true that the Arab world has achieved progress in many fields, as has been noted. However this progress is patchy, with differential development between Arab countries, and even within the same country. Despite undoubted advances, UNESCO figures show that almost two-thirds of the world's 792 million illiterate adults are women and more than 72 million girls at primary and secondary school age were not enrolled in a school in 2009. At the same time women have benefited from significant advances in health and education over the last fifty years. However, these gains are not reflected in a commensurate rise in employment and political representation. The economic and political engagement of Arab women continues to languish among the lowest in the world. This is due to various social, cultural and economic factors, including low economic growth, a weak labour market, legal constraints, as well as social arrangements, customs and traditions. In countries where there are greater opportunities for paid work for women, they are mostly to be found in the health, education and services sectors.

Women also suffer from low levels of representation in political parties and workers' trade unions. The empowerment of women thus still requires considerable effort, which must go beyond symbolic appointments to include genuine influence over decision making and policy formation. Gender equality is inseparable from social and economic progress, and it is essential to revise legislation to bring it into line with international declarations on women's rights that Arab countries have ratified, or in whose favour they have voted at the United Nations. Then obstacles must be removed in some Arab countries that prevent women from buying land, owning their own businesses or obtaining credit. Nor should maternity leave be an obstacle to female employment.

Although women are more liable to be unemployed than men, the lack of gender equality is also apparent in other ways, such as the gap in wages, professional isolation and the over-representation of women in the black economy. Here women have become especially invisible economically because they produce and sell commodities at home.

Which brings us to the unregulated black economy – another intractable problem facing the official economy as it seeks to improve the quality of production and stimulate economic growth.

Work in the black economy is characterised by low skill levels, low productivity and low or irregular incomes, combined with long hours of work in unsafe and unhealthy conditions, a shortage of information, and poor access to markets, financing, training and technology. Its exponents include porters, itinerant hawkers and street sellers of fruit and vegetables, meat, fish, fast food and a multitude of other items. The least visible are those tucked away in small commercial premises and workshops for such things as bicycle repair, scrap metal recycling, furniture making, leather tanning, shoemaking and repair, textile weaving and dyeing, tailoring, gem-polishing, and a host of other tasks. Then there are casual workers in restaurants and hotels, janitors and caretakers, temporary office personnel, and manual labourers who are either casual or work for a daily wage in the building and agricultural sectors.

Although these informal toilers constitute an entire economy parallel to the official one, they lack official recognition. Their invisibility means that they are not registered, taxed, organised or protected in accordance with labour and social security legislation, and so they are unable to exercise or defend their basic rights. Such workers are often excluded from education and health care, and they drift into life in and around the towns, placing a huge economic and social strain on the municipalities and the state, exacerbating problems such as sexual harassment, corruption, bribery and so on. Furthermore the commodities and services supplied by the unofficial economy are of low quality because they are not governed by legal and procedural requirements, such as registration of the businesses and quality control.

Inadequate housing and food for the informal labour force, unsafe drinking water and poor sanitary facilities, dangerous working environments and the lack of health care all contribute to poor health, amounting to a fundamental brake on growth and an intensification of poverty. Poor health means a reduced ability to work, reduced productivity and low life expectancy. Child labour and the exploitation of children in the black economy leads to them being denied education and perpetuates household poverty. It impedes economic growth and social development, and is in any case a glaring and criminal violation of children's rights.

The growth of the black economy is the result either of a failure to implement laws and policies correctly and effectively, or of the existence of inappropriate and ineffective legal and institutional frameworks. Many activities in the black economy demonstrate a high level of dynamism and inventiveness, but they operate outside the law and lack official sanction.

In order to avoid the snare of the black economy, a strategic policy must be put in place to integrate it gradually into the official economy. But this must be done without destroying opportunities to make a living and crushing the spirit of enterprise of those working in it. This requires identifying and treating the root causes of the problem, and this in turn requires massive investment in training and education, and also policies to counteract its disconnection from the official economy. The regulatory frameworks controlling the economy at large must be gradually reformed and expanded. This applies, for example, to commercial and economic regulations enacted to ensure a competent public administration that is accountable and free from corruption. This is of crucial importance for the growth of the private sector both domestically and abroad. The management of the labour market is a shared responsibility between governments, private sector institutions, and employees through their trade unions. These three parties must take up the responsibility of establishing, amending and applying the rules governing labour and related issues.

There is also a need to increase investment in the basic infrastructure and legal procedures that Arab countries require – for transportation and communications, for the management of water and sewage facilities, for power generation and supply, for environmental sustainability, for the co-ordination of commercial policies and procedures to eradicate inconsistencies, and for mechanisms for the settlement of disputes and conflict resolution.

Whereas poverty, unemployment and internal migration pose major challenges to countries such as Morocco and Egypt, in Iraq and Palestine the foremost issues centre on conflict resolution, the ending of occupation, the building of effective public institutions, the strengthening of civil society and the stimulation of economic growth. Algeria, Somalia and Sudan also continue to suffer from terrorism and internal strife, whereas in the Gulf States the issue of sustainability, whether economic, environmental or social, is of crucial importance and calls for action to predict and protect the future.

Despite disparities in progress, Arab countries face a common set of challenges that include peace and security, the resolution of the Palestinian issue, poverty reduction, economic growth, the establishment of comprehensive regional and Mediterranean joint ventures, respect for human rights, the implantation of real democracy and sound government, and environmental protection. The economic summit in Kuwait held on 19–20 of January 2009 addressed all of these issues (see Appendix 1).

We cannot turn a blind eye to the dispiriting fact that, at the beginning of the first decade of the third millennium, the Arab world was on record as having one of the lowest rates per capita of share in gross domestic product, reflecting its weak growth and slow progress in human development in comparison to the average for developing countries. This can be remedied only by increased productivity in all sectors of the economy, economic diversification and support for science and technology and innovation in those fields. It also demands a higher degree of regional integration, as was called for at the Kuwait summit meeting. The agricultural sector in particular demands increased investment in basic infrastructure, including the supply of water, energy and social services to improve farming incomes. There must also be encouragement for international and regional joint ventures that rely on mutual accountability and responsibility. Such joint ventures should focus on providing infrastructure for transportation, energy and water management, based on common strategies to respond to regional or global environmental issues. The integration of Arab markets into an Arab Common Market would make the region more attractive for international investors and create opportunities for work and income.

Democratic institutions remain weak and public institutions are still highly centralised. This restricts their ability to respond to the needs and concerns of the public. Much more must be done to ensure free and impartial elections, as well as civil liberties, press freedom, transparency, accountability, the rule of law, and complete separation between the legislative, executive and judicial arms of government.

When considering a charter of human rights, it needs to be remembered that the issue of refugees, displaced persons and migrant workers in the Arab countries has not attracted adequate attention. They are all exposed to marginalisation, discrimination and violation of their social, economic and civil rights.

There remains, finally, the perception that globalisation and the integration of the global economy represents the gravest threat facing Arab countries. So what is globalisation? What are its deficiencies? What are its benefits? What are its ethical values? We shall turn to these questions in the next chapter.

2

Globalisation: An Opportunity for a Real Arab Revival

B EFORE PLUNGING HEADLONG into globalisation, we should start by trying to define this modern political, economic and cultural term, and to explain its historical development and its current and future prospects. Let us start from the principle that human progress, whether it goes by the name of Classical, Islamic, revivalist, reformist, modernising, or indeed globalising, is no more the prerogative or monopoly of any single civilisation than is historical change in general. Any nation can participate in the forward march of the present by keeping abreast of it, by contributing to it through its own creative genius, or indeed by reacting against it.

Globalisation is fundamentally the accelerating process by which economies are integrated into a market arrangement of international scope. It consequently affects the basic functions of the economy, i.e. production, consumption and services, and its financial aspects, i.e. currency and capital.

During the Second World War and after, the Allies sought to reform the regulation of the international economy and to organise a return to free trade, by progressively removing the trade barriers between countries inhibiting the export and import of goods. The objective was to end the protectionism that had prevailed during the two world wars, and which had been a cause of the political friction culminating in the outbreak of hostilities.

Within the context of this effort the General Agreement on Tariffs and Trade (GATT), laying down the rules of the game on the fundamental principle of free trade, was ratified in 1947. Shortly before, in 1944, the international system of payment and currency exchange had been reorganised at the Bretton Woods Conference, resulting in the formation of the World Bank and the International Monetary Fund.

During the 1950s the process of internationalising economies took root and gradually expanded to cover not merely commerce in goods but also services such as banking and insurance. Major corporations moved capital around in the form of deposits or investments.

Following the collapse of the Soviet Union and the resulting acceleration of international trade, various Arabic terms were coined for globalisation. The current one, *'awlama*, appeared in the 1990s. Some people also call it *kawniyya*, in the sense of the integration of all national economies into a single universal economy.

Globalisation has had a profound impact on the market in goods, commodities, services, financial resources and the processes of production, from design, through execution, to completion. A number of commodities are still immune to its effects and have retained some degree of national protection. However the vast majority of commodities such as petroleum, computers, weapons, telecommunications equipment and the film industry have been fully globalised.

Globalisation is characterised by four main processes, not all of them as a result of globalisation itself, as follows:

1. The first, institutional in origin, was the succession of GATT agreements reducing customs tariffs, from 40 percent in the 1940s to 5 percent in the 1990s. This lowering of trade barriers, which

hitherto had hindered the international exchange of goods and commodities, contributed greatly to the growth of global trade.

2. The second process was the unpredicted development of electronics and computer technology during the last quarter of the 20th century. New telecommunications technology led to an exponential rise in information exchange and an explosion in the knowledge economy, as well as a reduction in the cost of freight, and breathed new life into banking and insurance services and the financial markets.

3. Third, the globalisation of production processes impacted on the strategies of major companies: they transformed themselves gradually into transnational corporations with offices and plant overseas. This development has led to no less than 40 percent of international trade being conducted between these major corporations.

4. The fourth effect derives from the restructuring of the international economic pecking order. From the end of the Second World War to the first petroleum crisis in 1974, the world economy could be divided into three groups: the United States and Canada, Western Europe and Japan, with developed market economies; the Communist Bloc covering the Soviet Union and Eastern Europe; and the Third World countries of Asia, Africa and Latin America. Following the collapse of the Soviet Union and as a result of the migration of manufacturing to various Asian and Latin American countries, new blocs appeared, dubbed the emerging economies, such as the Four Dragons of Asia – South Korea, Singapore, Thailand and Hong Kong – and subsequently the Seven Tigers of Brazil, China, India, Russia and other Eastern European and Latin American countries, with Egypt among them.

Of course the reach of corporations outside their countries of origin is hardly a new phenomenon, and the process can be traced back to the era of European empire and even before. Good examples are Shell (Dutch in origin) and BP (British), both of which began to drill for oil in other countries at the end of the 19th century. Other companies began to set up branches abroad after the Second World War, so becoming multinational. These were followed by truly global companies that appeared in the 1980s and developed global strategies for production and distribution with neither any consideration for the economic interests of the countries in which they operated, nor any loyalty to them. Nonetheless these multinational corporations were the force that spearheaded the globalisation of the economy.

As the marketplace became increasingly international, so too did taste, resulting in the standardisation of goods and commodities. Demand for products with a national or cultural flavour declined in the face of demand for global brands. Corporations and banks encouraged this trend through vigorous marketing campaigns via the press and media. Locally distinctive consumer goods have been swamped by demand for globally uniform products such as McDonald's, Levi's, Coca-Cola and so on.

The internationalisation of trade and the globalisation of capital movements have fuelled the growth of a new phenomenon. This is financial globalisation. Developed countries have ceased to apply national regulations, which has facilitated the formation of a unified global capital market, opening borders and enabling the free flow of capital around the world. This in turn has contributed to increased investment and economic growth and created new opportunities for work.

Financial globalisation has relied for its development on three factors. First, companies no longer need an intermediary bank to obtain loans for investment in new business activity because they are able to go directly to the financial markets. Second, the elimination of national regulations controlling the movement of capital from one country to another has led to the attainment of a key aim, the free flow of capital around the world. The third factor derives from corporations becoming increasingly flexible in the choice of market sector in which they seek investment, or intend to invest; this has enabled a movement from a monetary market to a securities market, from one share to another and from one currency to another in the search for profit and beneficial investment.

These factors have extended the scope of globalisation and have facilitated the flow of goods and commodities to achieve competition, and this in turn has stimulated the supply of commodities of high quality at ever lower prices. However they have also led to the collapse of the financial market, as we shall see in Chapter 6.

Among globalisation's major features are the speed of technological change, fluctuations in external demand, evolving forms of commercial exchange, intensified competition in both domestic and foreign markets, fluctuating flows of foreign investment, and changing patterns of migration. These features all put pressure on institutions to adjust and on the labour market to respond. Some safety measures are vital in the face of such disruptions: an environment conducive to the development of companies, labour market safeguards, and appropriate policies for restructuring commerce and industry. Such adjustments are needed to protect the wellbeing and dignity of the workforce and to generate high and stable rates of growth.

All economies have to adjust to ongoing fluctuations in production caused by varied rates of growth from one sector to another, changing technologies and forms of commercial exchange, and ups and downs in domestic demand. These factors interact with changes affecting the workforce, such as the growth in female employment and the unofficial workforce. An adequate response to these changes demands policies covering the encouragement of technological creativity, the restructuring of businesses, the supply of labour market data, up-skilling, effective social security provision, and effective mechanisms for social dialogue. The state must perform a decisive role in the formation of an institutional framework to harmonise the needs of business and workers with the ever-changing demands of the international economy.

We now live in a world in which the openness of national economies to global markets constitutes a threat to the political sovereignty of the state. Social dialogue can help with the choice of particular routes towards sustainable growth with a social dimension. Social dialogue of this kind will be able to aid recovery from financial shocks and provide safeguards against the occurrence of future disruption. Social dialogue and harmony reassures both domestic and foreign investors. The achievement of financial stability must not be at the expense of social and political stability.

No one can deny that one of the main challenges facing developing countries in general is to achieve and maintain some level and form of growth, hand in hand with a significant reduction of poverty.

However, this is threatened by the worldwide trend of economies to be ever-increasingly integrated, undermining purely national strategies aspiring to sustainable growth and seeking to provide employment and amelioration of the conditions of the poor. Strategies are essential that combine measures at a national level within the framework of an international effort to incentivise and support investment and the growth of trade. It is this combination that will lead to growth in the markets.

The volume of international financial flows and their instability, particularly in relation to investment in government bonds or in emerging financial securities markets, has caused wide fluctuations in exchange rates and interest rates, resulting in stunted growth.

International arrangements aimed at stabilising financial markets and opening up trade must be accompanied by measures at the national level to encourage growth and increase labour productivity. Increased productivity is the primary engine of sustainable growth, non-inflationary improvement in living standards and job creation. Increased productivity is brought about by updating production processes in order to reduce unit costs and by transforming products and services to deliver higher returns. Such growth will demand changes to the way in which labour is organised, the creation of new labour arrangements and the phasing-out of existing ones. Although many developing countries, advised by foreign consultants, have been seduced by expectations that strict financial and monetary policies will lead to the stability necessary for the stimulation of investment and growth, these results have been slow to appear. Rather it has been the case that social crises, disturbances and political difficulties arising from these policies have been obstacles in the way of determining a path to sustainable growth.

Hence one may ask: Is the state the biggest loser in the globalisation process? The management of the economy is no longer under its control. The state has lost ground to corporations, banks and international capital. The economies of advanced countries since the end of the Second World War have been distinguished by their mixed character as joint undertakings shared between the state and private enterprise. The state has undertaken the responsibilities of redistribution, regulation, and ownership and management of the public sector. Globalisation has turned this economic model upside down. The state has been weakened in favour of the market, and the market itself is no longer a national one as it has previously been. It has been inter-nationalised, and national decision-makers no longer exert influence over it.

The role of the state is now restricted to achieving an economic balance between job opportunities and economic growth, and to seeking an external balance by defending its interests in the face of other countries in the World Trade Organisation, the International Monetary Fund, and the G8, consisting of the eight major economies.

However the object of these international institutions is to put in place regulations to be imposed on all countries. They are in essence international co-operative institutions rather than supranational authorities. But they do enjoy some actual authority over the new operators in the international economy, that is, the transnational corporations, the major banks and the financial markets.

These countries, confronted with the globalising force that has deprived all states of a measure of their sovereignty, have turned to developing co-operative agreements among themselves within the framework of regional blocs that have become the connecting link between the national state and globalisation. These blocs have cushioned national economies against the adverse effects of globalisation by formulating common legal frameworks aimed at placing the market strategies of corporations on a legal footing. Among the most important of these blocs are the European Union with its economic and monetary integration; the North American Free Trade Agreement (NAFTA) consisting of the United States of America, Canada and Mexico; the MERCOSUR bloc consisting of Argentina, Brazil, Paraguay and Uruguay; the ASEAN or South East Asian bloc comprising ten countries; and the

SANGAY Co-operative Organisation that includes Russia, China, India and other Asian countries.

There is no doubt that the international economy needs to be rendered more humane. Legislation is required to make it more just, and there is a pressing need for national initiatives and reforms if the aim is to extend the opportunities and benefits afforded by globalisation to everyone in society.

To achieve this, national governments must take action in the following areas to help modernise the labour market:

1. Up-to-date information must be made available, through a network of employment agencies, on the skills, abilities and qualifications demanded by the whole spectrum of employers, from multinational companies to small businesses.

2. A flexible and effective technical and professional training programme must be established, combining both formal education and work experience, enabling job-seekers to respond to the changing requirements for skills and ability.

3. A sound collaborative framework, involving the state, trade unions and employers, must be set up to manage relationships in the workplace. The state must take responsibility for putting this in place, with rules to regulate trade union freedom, collective bargaining, working practices and conditions, wages, occupational health and safety, and business competitiveness.

4. The provision of social security systems and arrangements to combat social exclusion.

5. Integration between ministries in the adoption of economic, social and environmental measures.

6. Sound machinery of government based on democracy, social equality and the supremacy of law and human rights. There must also be effective collaboration and representation to meet the aspirations and interests of the main stakeholders, including workers, employers and the institutions of civil society. And there must also be moves to improve productivity in the black economy

and to absorb it into the official economy. Ensuring equal opportunities for all must be a major concern of good government everywhere.

We have to recognise that globalisation, despite its defects and evils, has brought considerable benefits to humanity. It has encouraged the free exchange of goods, ideas and knowledge, and has given much to societies that have opened up to the world. However an impartial verdict on globalisation is that it is engendering a crisis: there is a growing gulf between the economy, which has become increasingly international, and the social and political institutions within countries, which are losing their power to shape their societies – especially those governments which have not yet risen to the regional or international level. There is also a widening gulf between the international official economy and the spread of the local informal economy in most Arab countries. Most Arabs, who still live and work in the informal economy, are excluded from direct participation, on a fair and equal basis, in the official markets and thus in the benefits of globalisation.

Commerce and industry, especially in the West, have been freed up at a time when most Western countries continue to protect agriculture, although goods, commodities and capital still move freely across borders while the freedom of movement of people is restricted.

In order for globalisation to be better managed it is essential for it to adopt a new path giving priority to people, who are or should be the centre and focus of all economic development. A new course like this is one that some in the Arab world look upon as domination and exploitation in a new guise. Globalisation must take into account the social dimension, ensuring people have access to appropriate work and the basic necessities of food, water, health, education, housing and a safe environment. These things need to be brought to the fore. This can happen only if globalisation is administered within a proper democratic framework embracing involvement, accountability, the rule of law and respect for institutions, so providing a level playing field for national Arab policies to stimulate business development and work opportunities, to reduce poverty and guarantee gender equality. Conditions under which people can flourish enable them to develop their talent and ability, and will help each country to determine the best way forward in achieving its social and economic goals, in co-ordination and gradual integration with other Arab countries. Convergence in social and economic policies will contribute most to the penetration of globalisation and participation in better administration within the framework of the rule of law, parliamentary democracy, respect for the Treaty on Human Rights, and equality. Only the realisation of these conditions can be the basis for the integration of Arab countries into a fairer and productive globalisation, via their gradual economic absorption into a single Arab market. This was the reform called for by the Kuwaiti Economic Summit (Appendix 1).

Countries of the South fear the impact of globalisation on their cultural identity and local traditions. Countries of the North too have a fear: the rise of unemployment caused by the liberalisation of trade, investment and competition, because the higher cost of production inputs, including wages and the accumulation of social provision, has encouraged transnational corporations to seek out regions in the South where workers are exploited and paid trifling wages, and taxes and other costs are low because they include no provision whatsoever for social security.

To address the fear felt in countries of the South, globalisation must proceed in parallel with multiculturalism, because culture is a powerful symbol of identity, and the independence of national and local cultures must be recognised as a source of self-confidence and creative energy. There must be respect for cultural, religious, political and social diversity and a respect for human rights, dignity and gender equality. And respect for the natural world will help to make globalisation a force for environmentally sustainable growth.

As for the North, democratic rule fit for globalisation, an open market economy, responsible capitalism and initiatives, and respect for the law, integrity and transparency, will surely allay their fear of exporting their jobs to the South.

Open societies today are threatened by global terrorism, and the future of open markets is no longer guaranteed. Political challenges such as the Palestinian issue must be resolved if we are to create justice and reduce tyranny in our world. Terrorism feeds off powerlessness, deprivation, poverty and hopelessness in order to acquire legitimacy in the public mind. Such political and social conditions impede effective resistance to terrorism, because their victims lack the awareness and conviction to oppose it.

We can conclude from these observations that conditions for modernisation in the Arab world can be built through a creative interaction with globalisation, by taking advantage of its ingenuity and productivity and by acclimatising itself to new mechanisms of governance. An enlightened involvement in globalisation's civilising aspects will be liberating, allowing Arab countries a taste of democratic values and enabling them to participate in the progress of modernity. It will awaken them to humanity's essential unity and to the idea of international citizenship, and will bring a voluntary acceptance of the ethical, legal and economic responsibilities arising from these ideas. Mutual support and justice are values common to the whole of mankind. They are based on a fundamental natural law at the centre of any equitable social structure, which is freedom. Freedom lights the path to globalisation; without it we will travel along the way not out of choice, but as followers, because it is freedom that will release our powers of invention, and enable us to compete in the race for betterment.

That said, true freedom requires maturity and the acceptance of responsibility. In this context the exercise of freedom requires respect for moral duties in work and productive life, whether in the public or private sector. The next chapter will deal with these moral duties and values, and the professional and personal ethical standards that must be espoused.

3

Moral Responsibilities

W E LIVE IN A WORLD in which social status and respect stem from
our occupation and income. How others regard us, and how we
see ourselves, are closely linked to our jobs and how we are treated at
work. Labour is not just a commodity. People have a right to be treated
with respect.

The extent to which people feel they are fairly treated affects their
performance at work. Employers are aware that fair outcomes raise
morale, reduce employee turnover and absenteeism, and increase
productivity. A sense of injustice is the basis of all workplace grievances.
When there is fair treatment, performance improves.

Arab societies today are more mature and critical than they used to
be. They demand efficient, speedy, high-quality services from the state
and public sector. People expect civil servants to set a good example.
Professional ethics are the only means by which citizens' trust in the
administration can be restored. Reform is essential if employees are to
become mature, responsible functionaries with both rights and duties.
Sadly this is not the case in the Arab world. Wages and conditions of

public service in many Arab countries have declined sharply during the long years of austerity, restructuring and the debt crisis. All this has undermined morale and performance, which in turn has led to a loss of talent to the private sector and has encouraged the practice of officials charging citizens for carrying out their duties by demanding bribes. The result is a slump in confidence in government, so that it is commonly said, "Private good, public bad!"

Whatever balance is desired between public and private sectors, it is vital for state employment arrangements to be properly regulated. The public sector must be adequately financed if high-quality services are to be made available to all who need them. Public servants must be well-trained experts in their field. The civil service must develop the ability to promote social objectives, in particular the elimination of poverty and the provision of security and welfare. It must make a public pledge to apply the strictest professional ethics to the fulfilment of these aims. This will help the economy, in both its national and global aspects, to operate effectively and fairly. It will also ensure that workers in the public sector enjoy basic rights and proper working conditions.

Even though a high proportion of government spending is already allocated to salaries, resources must be increased to counter the problems of the public service and to oil the wheels of progress by ongoing negotiation and consultation with staff associations. Poor working conditions and continual delays in the payment of wages put a brake on the attainment of efficiency.

A debate on proposals to privatise basic public services is especially important in view of their strategic development status in the economy. There is no doubt that the existence of an impartial, competent and stable public service constitutes a major national resource for the provision of more and better education and health services.

Training is the starting point for reforms aimed at raising the standard of public services. It is vital to improve the performance of state-owned industries and to prepare them for privatisation and competition in global markets. Plans for such basic restructuring must take into account the social impact on surrounding communities, by dealing with the issues arising from expanding or reducing the workforce.

Social dialogue is a valuable tool in reaching agreement on modernising labour laws and formulating policies required to improve performance in the public sector and regulated private businesses.

So much for generalities about aims. As a point of entry into the detail of how to achieve them, we shall start with a round-up of the responsibilities, values and professional ethics that should govern public employment, the role of the state, and the criteria for reform. By public employees we mean all those holding a civilian post within a government body, whatever the nature of their work or job title.

A generally moral outlook is an essential characteristic of government employees, responsible as they are for the public interest. Correct behaviour is a prerequisite for anyone entrusted with the public powers conferred by their job, as are an unsullied reputation and the absence of any criminal record of dishonesty or other wrongdoing.

Civil servants can be placed in various categories according to job description, type of responsibility, type of work, and level of qualifications. Public positions, whether permanent or temporary, can be divided by hierarchy into those of management, office work, trades, and services. By professional ethics we mean a code of practice applicable to every job that should determine the behaviour of the employee. As a philosophical concept, this can be traced back at least as far as the ancient Greeks, in particular to the Hippocratic Oath in the 5th century BC.

During the 19th century various intellectuals set about establishing new basic principles as a foundation for professional ethics. As a result, engaging in a profession or any kind of employment entailed abiding by a set of rules and duties. In the event of an infringement, a panel empowered to enforce the code of ethics, acting as a judicial tribunal, would be responsible for disciplinary proceedings and penalties. These might range from a mere rebuke to suspension from work for a period of anything from two weeks to three months, or actual dismissal.

A code of professional ethics is a fundamental element of the self-governing professions such as medicine, law and engineering. It is a response to the insistence of society on monitoring and maintaining standards in those professions, to avert chaos. It also springs from the professions themselves, anxious to achieve public trust by means of an unimpeachable ethical standard. In the civil service it is the state that is the guarantor of such standards, curbing a free-for-all and applying disciplinary regulations in the event of violation. Spheres of work lacking a code of professional ethics are bound by and subject to the general criminal and civil law and administrative regulations.

The theory of moral responsibility hence ordains that politicians, civil service managers and employees fulfil their roles with integrity and respect for the principles of their calling. An official has an obligation above all to set a good example for others to follow. Next, he must adopt procedures appropriate to his particular level to ensure the proper functioning of his service, and to enable his staff to perform the tasks entrusted to them.

Values and objectives of a code of ethics

The main aims of a code of professional ethics are, first, to provide explicit guidelines setting out the rights and responsibilities of staff when going about their business. Secondly, it provides a useful yardstick for the management and monitoring of staff behaviour, and additionally provides protection for them from external influences. Thirdly, it fosters a culture of ethical behaviour so that it becomes the norm, and makes a positive contribution to the quality of working life.

The moral values of public service apply in practical terms to the relationships between public employees and their human environment. The particular nature of this situation is that a public servant deals with the public and with work colleagues within a staff hierarchy, while at the same time respecting the national or local political authority and implementing its decisions. This means that the values of the public service apply to his relationships with three groups, that is with the public, with work colleagues, and with the political authorities.

A code of practice would thus be based on the following values:

1. A permanent guarantee and adoption in all circumstances of human rights, freedoms and dignity.

2. A repudiation of any form of discrimination, whether towards citizens or employees.

3. The exercise of public authority with integrity and probity. Probity does not only mean combating corruption and favouritism. It also entails fairness, the personalisation of service, and professional competence and trustworthiness. Probity means more than merely respecting and applying the law. The administration must also set an example, and the public must have confidence in it and its representatives.

4. Proper performance. This principle means that the tasks assigned to the functionary are prepared constructively and in accordance with stated objectives, and that they are performed with initiative within the framework of respect for legality.

5. Confidentiality. This principle does not mean that officials are denied freedom of expression or freedom to exchange information with their colleagues and defend their ideas and proposals. Nor should it prevent citizens from being provided with the information they request. Rather the intention is that the authority should have the right to restrict freedom of expression where this serves the public interest, for example in matters of security or public order.

Professionalism and respect for the dignity of their position demand the following standards from employees:

1. Avoidance of behaviour unworthy of the profession, such as indecent dress, abusive language, backbiting or slander against work colleagues.

2. Readiness to perform their work professionally and competently at all times – the quality of their work relies heavily on their professional approach.

3. Good time-keeping and commitment to the tasks entrusted to them, and willingness to assist those using their services.

4. Respectful and trustworthy use of telecommunications, according

to the needs of the job. Here too the management must respect employees' private life.

5. Avoidance of alcohol, drugs or medicines during working hours, other than on medical grounds, because they are banned and have a negative impact on job performance.

When an employee has dealings with staff in another organisation, or with the public or some other outside body, the following standards apply:

1. If the purpose is to provide a service to a colleague, every effort must be made to do it as well as possible, with a sense of personal obligation, whether the user is a citizen, official, or employee of another services sector.

2. Coercion for unlawful reasons must not be used. To force people to do things in this way demands censure and must be punished. Compulsion should be used only when it is lawful and essential.

3. Quality service provision must be a collective operation, from the bottom to the top, in organisation, service and management.

4. Integrity. Employees must not obtain benefits to which they are not entitled, and must refrain from pilfering and misusing facilities at their disposal.

5. Impartiality. Political, philosophical or religious convictions, or access to political influence, must not interfere with employees' dealings with colleagues or the public. A public servant must therefore avoid dealing with cases in some way connected with him.

6. Respect for privacy. Secrets and information related to citizens' private life must not be disclosed, in order to safeguard their physical, mental and social wellbeing.

7. Access. The administration and civil servants must be approachable, and respond to citizens' questions and provide the services they need.

8. Accountability. Every civil servant is responsible for the work

entrusted to him and must be ready to give an account of his actions.

As for the employee's relationships within his own organisation, he must contribute to a positive working atmosphere by respecting his colleagues and refraining from inappropriate behaviour. He must also be prepared to work as part of a team and have confidence in his workmates. He must be open with them and discuss potential problems in a positive and constructive manner.

Without doubt the management hierarchy, the staff's respect for it and how it behaves all contribute significantly to a conducive work atmosphere. Senior management has a basic obligation to uphold the values and principles of the organisation's code of practice. In return, employees must respect the leadership by doing their jobs and giving due acknowledgement to the work of senior management. Any disputes between management and employees on working methods must be resolved by consultation and dialogue between the individuals concerned.

Professional values

The civil service cannot fulfil its role unless its staff are characterised by true professionalism. Professional values in the public sector differ not at all from those applicable to the private sector. Common to both are a high-quality work ethic in which professionalism is based on a combination of legality, efficiency, transparency, independence, appropriateness, continuity and integrity. All staff-members should set a good example to others through their loyalty to the organisation and commitment to the team effort.

A good civil servant must possess the following characteristics:

1. Respect for the law. This must permeate every aspect of the public employee's work. Law-abiding government exists to enforce the legislation voted upon by representatives of the people. The civil servant as an agent of government has a public trust to abide by the law and to guarantee legality, which he shares with his

superiors and subordinates. They are required in all things to ensure their decisions are in accordance with the law and their formulation in accord with normal procedures.

This law-abiding aspect also includes loyalty to fellow-officials and to the elected authorities in the employee's organisation.

Although civil servants have the right to freedom of opinion and expression when at work, they do not have the right to impede legitimate decisions on the basis that they do not conform to their personal views. They must also respect professional confidentiality.

2. Effectiveness. This standard requires an official to aspire to an ever-higher level of professionalism and not to be swamped by bureaucracy. He should promote improvement in the quality of service and should always pursue personal and collective achievement. The management should provide him with satisfactory working conditions and give him the opportunity to attend professional training courses.

Effectiveness is no more than theoretical and subjective unless linked to proper assessment on the basis of objective criteria. The development and spread of a culture of assessment is fundamental for measuring the effectiveness of services provided. Effectiveness as a professional standard is linked to other standards such as quality, transparency and independence.

3. Responsibility. Administrative laws in almost all countries contain provisions specifying this fundamental professional standard, which requires employees to perform their duties and fulfil their obligations as servants of the public interest. Responsibility also demands accountability: that employees provide reports on their work to both the political authority and to the public. Accountability of this kind is the best guarantee of respect for the values of public service and public positions of employment.

4. Quality. This is the best guarantee of effectiveness. It enhances professionalism and benefits the public. It is essential that it too is assessed as a service to the public.

5. Transparency. This is a new professional standard that has become a hallmark of modern developed societies. However it can come into conflict with some needs of government, and also with professional confidentiality.

6. Independence. The public sector in most countries still treats citizens as if they were employees rather than consumers, by applying the letter of the law and dealing with them in an over-officious bureaucratic manner. The private sector is more flexible: it quickly adapts to social expectations, such as the ever-increasing individualism that is bringing about a new and more consumerist citizenship. The private sector has also begun to fulfil its social responsibilities towards its workforce and to take action in favour of sustainable growth, respect for the environment and combating pollution.

   In the same way the public sector must abandon its current rigidity. It has become the right of every operator of a public service, whether a school or hospital or social service, to enjoy a measure of independence from authority enabling it to respond effectively and adapt to new demands. Relative independence for the public sector will engender public services more able to adjust to social changes and to build relationships with the public.

7. Adjustment. The administrative law in most countries assumes that public services will adjust continuously to keep abreast of the changing needs of society. But the administration itself is the decision-maker when it comes to determining the time and method of adjustment to changes. So adjustment as a professional standard must be understood in a broader sense than its definition in the administrative law. It means constant renewal, taking into consideration changes in social behaviour and technological progress. For example a department could open on a public holiday to adjust to electronic changes. This approach must develop in response to actual circumstances, and it should also include the professional life of employees. It is essential to separate positions of employment from status so that the management can

appoint employees to perform jobs and tasks that are appropriate for the needs of the public services without this affecting the employee's status in society.

Adjustment also means anticipating the consequences of a decision or policy. As noted above, companies in the private sector have added sustainable growth to their strategies, so for how long will the public service fail to keep abreast of this new trend? Especially as the public are waiting most patiently for the civil service to respect standards for the environment and integrate sustainable growth targets into its behaviour and decision-taking.

8. Continuity and stability. Continuity requires the state to defend itself against external aggression, protect its citizens, guarantee their physical safety, actively supply their basic needs, and in general maintain social cohesion. It also means concern for those who lose their jobs as a result of public organisations dispensing with their services.

9. Integrity. When the civil service imposes such measures as tax collection, tariffs on goods, expropriation for the public good, or travel restrictions, it will find such things are unacceptable to the public unless they genuinely serve the public interest. They are completely unacceptable if the objective is to serve private interests.

The level of corruption in public administration is incontestably the best indicator of the democratic health of any country. Citizens therefore rightly insist on the probity of the civil service and the integrity of the powers that be.

Integrity is a broader concept than probity. It cancels out all personal interest when a particular issue is being dealt with. Officials must perform their work faithfully, honestly and impartially, and must not be led astray by their own ego or personal interest.

10. Setting a good example. A public servant will set a good example if he respects the values above and is guided by them in his work. He must set the standard for others. Lower functionaries cannot

be expected to behave properly if the top of the pyramid fails to show the way. "If the head of the household beats the drum, everyone in the house will dance."

The civil service must begin first of all by practising what it preaches, and applying its regulations to itself before imposing them on others. For example, if it does not enforce the law requiring the employment of disabled people in a specific proportion within the public administration, it is not sensible for it to punish the private sector for not applying it.

Furthermore the culture of respect within the civil service and its organisations must be developed. Cultivating obedience within the hierarchy demands that senior staff and managers take into account the personal circumstances of their subordinates. It presupposes that the relationships between the two sides are not restricted to the issuing and enforcement of orders. A culture of listening and understanding is fundamental in the achievement of good and effective management of human resources.

The interface with the public, whether in person, by telephone, by post or electronic mail, will demand certain standards – for example courtesy, accessibility, alacrity and clarity of response, accompanied by a willingness to listen, patience and transparency. Officials must show enthusiasm and explain to citizens, politely, what the law permits and does not permit, or what does or does not serve the public interest. This does not mean that officials should accept every member of the public's request. What it does mean is that they should show solidarity with the needy and poverty-stricken, and offer them help within the law and in accordance with public welfare. Solidarity also entails developing team spirit with colleagues to combine individual and collective effectiveness. It embraces both superiors and subordinates, especially when others are facing a problem that is difficult for them to handle without support.

Human and professional values and reform

An employee is not just a unit of labour, an exponent of efficiency, professionalism and performance, a mere instrument of his department.

He is first and foremost a human being with the right to be himself and express his human values. A civil servant has a mission to see, to hear, to cure and to govern. All of this demands an empathy with his fellow man that transcends his professionalism, if his handling of the public is to rise to this high human standard. However, an employee must be able to distinguish between his own personal ethical beliefs on the one hand, and the law and his moral duty to society on the other. For example it is not his job to give lessons in personal ethics to citizens. He must constantly bear in mind that his first duty is to abide by the law. Empathy with the individual has its place provided it remains within the law.

The aim of ethics, in this personal sense, is the achievement of a good way of life for oneself, at home and at work, based on justice, wisdom and respect for other individuals. Moral duty has a wider sense, being social rather than personal, and includes professional values. Its aim is to achieve discipline and collective co-operation.

Personal ethics are a matter of the individual working out the best ways to co-exist with other individuals. They depend on an ability to tell right from wrong. However moral philosophy shows us that feelings that are good and humane do not necessarily result in action that is lawful. For example an employee who imposes his sincerely held religious, personal or political ethics on his colleagues can quickly transmogrify into a rabble-rouser in his department. In this case it is the role of the law to protect the public from any backward personal ethics indulged in by civil servants.

The success or status of a civil servant in his community, outside work, can be quite independent of his wider moral duty to society. For example, he may be a greedy self-seeker or a liar, or he may misrepresent situations or engage in doublespeak, all of which contravene his moral duty but enable him to be a notable in his community. However these are most certainly counterproductive qualities in his job.

Hence right conduct is not necessarily a recipe for social or political advancement. Better to regard it as an art for its own sake, the art of duty towards others. Civil servants should treat their calling as an art form and do their duty without ostentation: efficiency without superfluity requires finesse, as do avoiding mistakes, fulfilling the demands of one's job, and doing the right thing by one's colleagues and the public.

Right conduct at work is an explicit professional requirement that is monitored, and wrongdoing is punishable in various ways depending on the legal status of the job and the methods of enforcement available.

Right conduct in the private sector is the same as in the public sector, demanding integrity and professional independence in its employees and the eradication of conflicts of interest.

Having said all that, in assessing the performance of the civil service, personal ethics must play a role in its culture second only to professionalism. The service must treat the public with respect, and its handling of business must be objective and equitable, whether with its staff or citizens. Absolute neutrality towards both politicians and the public must be its watchword.

In exchange for this, staff must abide by their job descriptions and refrain from activities conflicting with their moral duty. They must serve the public interest, actively apply the law and regulations, and obey their superiors' instructions. They must transact the business of interested parties faithfully and honestly.

Regulations prohibit employees from disclosing information gained by virtue of their position unless the management permits it. Such controls underline the principle that a civil service post is both a task and a trust, whose purpose is to serve the public. A person holding such a post must be fully conversant with its responsibilities and fulfil them diligently and personally, without delegating them to others.

While an employee may engage in private work outside official working hours for payment, he must avoid work detracting from the dignity of his official position. It is not permitted to hold down two jobs within the administration.

To maximise staff performance their abilities must be known and put to best use by an appropriate distribution of assignments, and attention to their working environment and their needs and aspirations. They must be given proper guidance, helped with resolving any personal problems, and incentivised by rewards for initiative and success and by penalties for shortcomings.

Dissatisfaction among staff not receiving the same salary and incentives as similar employees at same level of responsibility in other bodies must be avoided.

The creation of posts for the sake of providing employment instead of employing staff to fill vacant posts must also be avoided. This creates financial obligations outside the budget and diverts funds allocated for other vital purposes.

There should be more seminars for senior administrators on how to assess the management's performance and the need for new skills. Senior administrators must participate in these training programmes and of course adequate resources must be budgeted for this purpose. Training should not be confined to employees but must include the leadership too, to avoid a gap opening up between the new skills of the department and the lagging ability of an untrained leadership.

Some departments have established disciplinary boards to punish employees who do not live up to the requirements of their job or who are guilty of dereliction of duty.

These boards impose disciplinary penalties, according to special regulations for each category of employee designed to provide a guarantee of consistent treatment. They include provisions for caution and reprimand, deduction of salary, suspension for a specified period, dismissal from the post or the service, compulsory retirement, and dismissal including withholding of all or some pension rights or redundancy payments.

Such disciplinary procedures guarantee fair and equal treatment of similar cases. They bring consistency to the conduct of the investigation, the right to study the evidence, the right of defence and the right of appeal. An employee may not be punished before an investigation has been conducted in writing, and a decision to impose a penalty must state the reasons for it.

Disciplinary accountability results from an employee violating his terms of employment. Criminal accountability results from perpetrators breaking the law of the land. Disciplinary punishment adversely impacts a person's employment and has financial and intangible consequences. Criminal punishment affects the individual's whole life, his freedom and possessions.

Management relies on reports assessing employees' competence to identify any shortcomings, with a view to remedying them. These reports also serve as a basis for promotion and reward. The assessment must take into account the seniority of the post, not the salary grade. This requires a separation between management and technical positions.

In order to regulate the relationship between management and employees, there have to be rules and regulations in place that aid the resolution of management problems. A tribunal will hear the extent to which disciplinary punishments may or may not fit the gravity of the offence or degree of dereliction of duty. The tribunal may also hear employees' grievances against reports on their competence and against denial of promotion, in the light of the employee's representations and in accordance with general rules. This body may be thought of as an administrative court.

Among the factors inspiring employees' commitment and dedication to the service is a feeling of security and a sense that their aspirations are being fulfilled by both financial and less tangible gains. Promotion always intensifies these feelings and should be a genuine reward for genuine effort. So rules for awarding promotion and criteria for monitoring them must be put in place. Promotion must be granted on the basis of true worth and performance. Seniority, competence and academic qualifications should also be taken into account. The temptation to make exceptions and break the rules in favour of individual cases must be resisted at all costs. Promotion gained through undue influence and nepotism causes disenchantment and frustration among those lacking such advantages, so damaging the public interest.

Then there is the question of reviewing wages, salaries and allowances to meet the rising cost of living caused by intractable crises in most Arab countries. If and when they carry out such reviews, their regimes, with the exception of those in the Gulf States, fail to take into account the dramatic fluctuations in prices and other changes caused by globalisation. Measures currently being taken to deal with this situation are in no way adequate to the scale of the problem. Trifling increases in pay are no answer to the terrifying rise in the cost of living. Radical remedies are needed for this malaise, which has fuelled unbridled bribery and corruption, undermined efficiency everywhere, increased poverty, and encouraged the expansion of the black market. Civil servants must be warned of the danger of disclosing confidential information or selling it to financial markets or property speculators. Sometimes such information even has a bearing on national security, making confidentiality in the public service a prime condition of trustworthiness.

Confidentiality demands particular care and attention when speaking in public places or on the telephone. Care must be taken not to leave important files or documents in offices, and not to take them home, carry them in private vehicles or dispose of them in waste bins. The circulation and monitoring of correspondence must also be carried out with care, from printing to delivery. It is wrong to disclose a professional or administrative secret even if the person told of it is a colleague working in the same department. Being party to secret information can harm the person or persons sharing it.

As with confidentiality, so with obedience, which is also among the values requiring special nurture. Obedience stemming directly from the hierarchy of the service is obligatory for all employees regardless of their rank or grade. It is an essential quality in both public and private sectors. It is fundamental to building confidence and leaving nothing to chance. A manager who does not trust his staff or who cannot rely on them is responsible for a service that can only deteriorate.

There are various complications centring on the concept of obedience. The first concerns who is to be obeyed. Should an official do only what his immediate superior instructs him to do? What about obedience to the heads of other departments?

Obedience has to be considered in the context of the working environment only, and should be assumed not to be extended into other spheres. For example it would be wrong for a consultant to obey a minister unless the work context demands it and there is an official regulation to that effect. Should a manager be obeyed if he acts in violation of the law or regulations?

Therefore the duty of obedience presupposes that the work of employees and officials is above reproach and has been approved by monitoring and assessment. Employees in both public and private sectors must be ever on the lookout to combat three dangers. The first is any threat to public health, for example contaminated blood. The second is deception perpetrated on the public, such as concealing deficiencies in the service provided. The third is placing personal benefit above public welfare.

Deception can take the form of an official hiding information from his boss. For example, the boss may be the last person to learn of a project dear to the official's heart. Or else the official may claim that such-and-such an opinion is the manager's, or he may fail to defend the department's considered view by attributing it to someone else in the department. An official may get his boss to sign negative letters while retaining the positive ones for his own signature. He may present attractive proposals to his colleagues or to his trade union and put his boss in the position of having to reject them. Or he may allow a mistake to be disclosed while well-aware of the embarrassment that might ensue, or without notifying his seniors to that effect.

The deceit of an employee typically passes through four stages:

1. Hiding information from his immediate superior or delaying its reaching him.

2. Mendacity.

3. Covert and persistent criticisms of the behaviour and tendencies of his superior.

4. Insubordination and deeming his superior to be incompetent to manage.

Finally, a degree of egomania gives rise to two types of deviance in public office. First is an official's self-important belief that the projects that he himself finds desirable and attractive should be implemented, even if this serves the interests of an opponent or competitor. Sometimes the worship of efficiency adds fuel to this deviance.

Second, self-aggrandisement conflicts with the ethos of public office, which entails that employees should suppress personal feelings and inclinations and keep their aspirations to themselves. Personality is inimical to administration. It generally becomes visible only in the signature. Hence the administrative machine prefers to use the third person in letters, such as "It is appropriate" or "It appears that", and it avoids the use of the first person.

Managers nonetheless expect personal allegiance from their subordinates. As a quid pro quo it is important that the subordinate feels validated by being allowed to express his personal opinion on a project that has been formulated by someone else. In line with this approach the signature indicates a decision and responsibility, and should not be seen as a means of self-promotion.

Finally, an official may be invited to participate in a conference. Such invitations typically fall into one of three catagories:

1. He is invited to be principal speaker, in which case his expenses should be paid by the organiser on the same basis as the other speakers'.

2. He is invited as a speaker, but not the principal one. His participation in this case should be decided on by his line manager.

3. He is invited to attend as an observer. In this case his participation must be at the expense of his employer or at his personal expense, and any offer by the organiser to pay his expenses should be refused.

The trade union rights of employees

In many countries moral duties have been incorporated either into administrative laws or into statute or the law of the land. Trade union rights for employees like other laws emerged originally from concepts of natural rights and moral theory. In the civil service the administrative departments are able to request the trade union to authenticate the representative capacity of its officials, namely that a trade union official has been elected, has paid his subscriptions and enjoys senior rank, experience and influence, and that he is independent of his department and is of sound moral standing.

The function of a trade union is to demand that appropriate

conditions of work are adhered to, such as working hours, overtime, daily and weekly breaks, holidays, retirement and pension rights, health and safety guarantees for employees, wage negotiation procedures, and continuing professional development and training. Employees' basic rights are freedom of opinion and association, the right to strike, and the right to be indemnified by the administration against legal action arising from direct professional error or the nature of the employment.

In exchange for this employees and their trade union must respect their moral obligations, in particular the duties of obedience, discipline, respect for the hierarchy, integrity, trustworthiness, loyalty, confidentiality, and notifying officials of criminal violations. Employees bear criminal responsibility in the event of their endangering life, even when this is unintentional. They also bear criminal responsibility if they deliberately exceed their authority and breach the duty of integrity, for example through corruption, influence peddling, betraying professional secrets, or serving personal interests in an unlawful manner.

Disciplinary punishments vary from one country and culture to another and according to the laws in force in each state. However they mostly have two elements in common. First, the accused has the right to defend himself and examine his file. Second, the prevalent disciplinary measures are usually of four levels of severity. First comes a caution or reprimand, or withholding of promotion. The second level involves reduction of pay grade, and temporary suspension for two weeks or more. A third level of sanction comprises demotion, and suspension for between three months and two years. The fourth and harshest level of punishment comprises compulsory retirement and dismissal. This requires there to be dual legal monitoring, to verify the legality and integrity of criminal penalties adopted by the disciplinary board or administrative court.

4

Sound Governance and Administrative Reform

H<small>UMAN SOCIETIES ARE WIDELY</small> disparate in character and mode of government, reflecting their historical experience, culture and religious values. No single model of government exists. Rather there are civilisations that have evolved through interaction with their various contexts and ways of doing things, while at the same time sharing values and principles common to them all. These values and principles have given rise to what we know today as the philosophy of moral obligation. Sound, successful government reconciles the various interests of stakeholders – owners, partners, shareholders, consumers, financiers, suppliers and contractors. The criteria for the harmonisation of such interests, which may often be conflicting, spring from an awareness of moral responsibility for the public interest, by means of dialogue between all those involved.

The state bears the basic responsibility for ensuring good, sound governance. This entails upholding the institutions of government, reforming public administration, improving administrative competence in both central and local planning, and fostering an institutional culture that guarantees transparency and combats corruption – all this in order to enhance both local and national economic potential in accordance with available economic resources – and then involving civil society and the private sector so that they can take their fair share of responsibility.

Sound government includes orderly planning and regulation of towns and districts to prevent random development, in consultation and co-operation with community organisations, people's associations, and district and village representatives, with the ultimate purpose of attaining sustainable growth. So sound government requires the state to uphold the law in the following areas:

1. Democratic government based upon genuine parliamentary participation, support for democratic institutions and civil society, sponsorship of human rights, and support for the legal framework of political parties and associations.

2. Administrative governance, entailing the improvement of working methods in public departments, enhanced co-ordination, consultation and co-operation between government ministries, the combating of fraud and corruption, the guarantee of transparency, all guided by a sense of moral responsibility.

3. Local government, which must be empowered to support rural and local development and the process of decentralisation.

4. Economic governance, which must pursue ever greater competence in managing the nation's economy and finance, and encourage the development of the private sector.

5. Public sector reform: a national programme for sound government that includes reform of the public administration, policies for the decentralisation of education and health, and the partial privatisation of some other public service utilities.

Sound governance in the private sector requires businesses to engage with their partners and take into account their social, cultural, economic and environmental surroundings. They must minimise risk, anticipate future obligations and adopt realistic strategies. They must also give due consideration to their non-material capital, that is, their human resources. This is vital in order to compete effectively and for good public repute. They must pursue policies to raise and maintain high standards and skills in their workforce.

There are four distinct aspects of government, though there must be co-ordination, interaction and integration between them. They have different methodologies but they bear joint responsibility for the management of their common affairs.

1. National government, which includes the various levels of local government. The state is responsible for the development of public departments, carrying out reforms and structural changes and adjustments, as well as for managing relations with other countries, and implementing economic and social policies. We shall return later to the role of the state in institutional reform.

2. Municipal and local government, which has its own special features, involving as it does co-ordination between stakeholders, social groups and institutions to attain particular objectives formulated at various stages of development and compromise between conflicting interests.

   Municipal government especially demands a framework for collective effort and strategic thinking that brings together the basic stakeholders at the political decision-making level. And local government needs to create conditions whereby citizens can contribute to projects at the formulation and appraisal stages.

   District and municipal government must develop collaboration between the public and private sectors, and ensure their shared responsibility for the management of public affairs in regions with a wide variety of needs and at different stages of development.

3. International governance, which involves the management of various forces: relations with other governments, with non-governmental bodies, with international and financial bodies, and with regional organisations. The aim of government at this level is to constantly renew the world order, arouse concern for the

environment, and to adapt the distribution of roles at international level to new and emerging geostrategic circumstances. This process demands co-operation between competing and sometimes conflicting interests. It is a complex maze for stakeholders in the world today. Mechanisms for decision-making and co-ordination, for example between members of the World Trade Organisation and non-members, are extremely weak.

4. Corporate governance, which covers global, intercontinental and multinational companies, public corporations and financial markets, and, in the private sector, medium-sized and small businesses, and the professions such as health, education and employment.

Corporate governance

This type of governance is typified by mechanisms of co-ordination and mutuality. It is a matter of integrating the authority of the shareholders, leadership and consumers with the responsibilities of the board of directors. Corporate governance is also characterised by a separation between management, control and monitoring. The pivotal relationships are those between the company management and the board of directors, the shareholders and other interested parties.

Corporate governance sets out the arrangements by which a company's ends and means are determined together with a commitment to monitor results. A company's quality depends upon its ability to incentivise its management and board of directors to pursue its aims in accordance with its own and its shareholders' best interests, as demonstrated by effective monitoring of the results achieved.

There is a difference between the Anglo-American and European models of corporate governance. The Anglo-American model focuses on the shareholders, that is, those who have taken the financial risk by investing, and who bear the brunt, or the profit, of that risk. The overriding objective is to maximise the company's value for the shareholders.

The European model involves a wider range of stakeholders. They have a financial share, thus lessening the return to regular shareholders. The aim of this is to protect the interests of all those with an interest in the company, namely employees, consumers, shareholders and management. Under this model the company is required to satisfy all those affected by its activities.

The board of directors is the body appointed to determine company policy. It monitors results over the long term, and is empowered to control the running of the company and its business activities. It is responsible for the appointment and dismissal of the chairman of the board and the general managers. It has the right of access to all necessary information. Collective leadership by the board is undoubtedly the crucial ingredient.

The board's other duties are as follows:

1. To issue and ratify the company accounts.
2. To convene the annual general meeting of the shareholders.
3. To appoint top managers.
4. To maintain the confidentiality of information provided to it.
5. To respond to written questions from shareholders during annual general meetings.

The function of the management is to apply the long-term policy and business strategy laid down by the board to the short-term running of the company, by managing its financial, human and technical facilities and resources. The management has to record its achievements in an annual report and endorse the final accounts. The function of top management is to provide quality leadership through its expertise, experience, network of relationships and its vision for the future, and not to be unduly swayed by daily events.

Corporate moral obligations

There can be no good corporate governance without moral values and moral authority, which impose integrity and proper conduct on individuals. Management plays a lead role in the propagation of values and awareness of moral responsibilities, which must be reflected in the activities of the company. The most important of them are the following:

- Avoidance of conflicts of interest.

- Avoidance of disclosing commercially sensitive information, and of exploiting it for personal gain.

- Ensuring transparency and accuracy in information supplied by those assisting the company's officials.

- Establishing relationships that serve the company's customers and facilitate the work of its suppliers, while avoiding accepting gifts and exercising due caution when responding to biased or suspect invitations.

- Due caution in building relationships with the managements of other companies and with the political sphere. It is incumbent upon the Chief Executive Officers of companies registered on the stock market to be aware of the public duties and obligations they must subscribe to before accepting their roles as CEOs.

It is the job of the CEO to have a thorough knowledge of his company's internal systems, legal requirements, procedural rules, moral responsibilities and general workings. This includes the modus operandi of the board of directors. It is a requirement for the CEO either already to be a personal shareholder in the company, or to buy shares when he takes up his duties. Nonetheless despite his own shareholding he represents all the shareholders. He must act in accordance with the company's best interests and allocate adequate time to his job.

If he performs executive functions in other companies, he must not do so in more than four of them, whether they are foreign or outside his own corporate group. It is his duty to notify the board if there is a conflict of interest or the possibility of one. Furthermore he must refrain from voting when matters arise conflicting with his own personal interests. It is also his duty as CEO to attend meetings regularly and to provide the chairman of the board with all appropriate and necessary data for the agenda, excluding only confidential professional information.

The CEO must on no account rely on unpublished insider knowledge when buying or selling the company's shares. All such transactions must be conducted by him strictly in accordance with the law and regulations in force.

There has to be a clear distinction between the role of the chairman of the board of directors and that of the CEO. It is preferable for the majority of the members of the board to be independent. It is the job of management to familiarise the board members with their role in line with the principles of moral responsibility and sound governance.

Certain governments have introduced important reforms in the area of company governance, especially for those registered on the stock market. Belgium, for example, has adopted a special set of principles of good corporate governance, as follows:

- Enunciation of a mission statement as a reference frame-work for the company's management.
- A recommendation to engage legal expertise from outside the company.
- Establishment of appropriate infrastructures for the guidance of management.
- The selection of a competent management team qualified to achieve the desired results.
- The fostering of shareholder commitment.
- Co-operation and effective interaction between the board of directors, the management and shareholders.

The governance of companies in Britain emphasises a system of management and monitoring that combines management efficiency with an assurance of trust for investors and security for the shareholders. In the reforms introduced by the British government at the end of the 1990s, there is a focus on strengthening the role of appointments committees and on the question of return on capital investment.

France made reforms at the beginning of this century as follows:

- All companies, whether registered on the stock exchange or not, must choose between having a board of directors or an executive board (directoire) comprising both monitoring and management.

- The functions of the chairman of the board of directors and the chief executive are to be clearly separated.

- All relevant information about the company must be disclosed to shareholders.

- The arrangements, work practices and membership of the board of directors must be periodically reviewed.

- There must be at least two independent members on the board.

- There must be an accounts committee and a committee for deciding dividends (return on capital).

Following the Enron, Anderson and WorldCom scandals at the beginning of this century, leading up to the Madoff Investment Scheme and similar debacles, a new law has been enacted in the United States compelling publicly quoted companies to provide accounts signed by the chairman of the board to the US Market Operations Review Committee (MORC). The new law also insists that the auditors must be independent of the company leadership, which applies equally to foreign companies operating in the US.

The reform measures instituted by the Chairman of MORC are as follows:

1. Directors are prohibited from being board members of more than two companies registered on the stock market.

2. The board of directors must meet at least eight times a year.

3. The board of directors must pay visits to all the company's premises.

4. Directors must undergo fresh training annually to increase their

understanding of the company and the sector in which it operates.

5. Directors are barred from keeping their positions on the board for more than ten years.

6. Directors' remuneration can no longer be in the form of stock options.

Reform of the public administration

Globalisation has led to a profound rethink about the role and functions of the state and has caused the principles and values hitherto thought necessary for the administration of public affairs to be brought under scrutiny. Professional values and the ethics underpinning them have become fundamental to work in both public and private sectors. Were we to ask an Arab or a European citizen to list for us the principles upon which an employee should base his actions, or that should form the bedrock of his sense of duty, they would both give a very similar reply, as has been shown by a number of social studies. These may be summarised as follows.

A desire for top-quality work; respect for consumers of public services; impartiality; a non-political management; integrity and dignity; devotion to the public interest; trustworthiness; loyalty to the institutions of state; confidentiality and due reserve; a positive attitude to serving the public; honesty and incorruptibility; an acute professional conscience; disapproval of carelessness and absenteeism; respect for the management hierarchy; competence; placing the public interest above the private; the development of a sense of responsibility; and a quest for fairness.

These spontaneous responses by citizens around the Mediterranean basin differ not at all in practical terms from the basic moral code that proclaims the duty of service to the public interest, professional reticence and confidentiality, the public right to full disclosure, and the obligation to do one's job properly, to faithfully carry out management instructions, to take on no more than one paid position at a time, and to monitor employees who move from the public to the private sector to ensure that no corruption, bribery or fraud is involved.

It is true that the scope of ethical values is wider than the legal code, in the sense that doing something ethically reprehensible does not necessarily amount to a violation of either the civil, criminal or commercial law. For example perfectionism, the desire to do a top-quality job, is an attitude of mind leading to a mode of behaviour. Falling short does not lead to punishment under the law. Ethical instincts and values lead us to frame codes of behaviour and ultimately laws, but an ethical system is not thereby the same thing as a legal system. Codes of professional behaviour are an aspect of moral duties that operate alongside the general civil, criminal and commercial legal system, but unlike the latter they do not necessarily entail punishments for those infringing them. In some countries the professions themselves have their own tribunals or disciplinary bodies to hold to account and penalise those who infringe the code.

Such then is the environment brought about by globalisation, especially after Ronald Reagan and Margaret Thatcher came to power in the US and Britain during the 1980s and initiated policies to review the role of the public sector and to reform the public service. These included the promotion of decentralisation to bring public institutions closer to the citizenry and to reduce the cost of organisational infrastructures. There was a new emphasis on keeping political ideology out of public administration, and safeguarding civil servants' independence, along with better-defined job descriptions for them and of the skills and competence expected of them, from which followed the need to increase the budgets allocated to professional training. Finally the exchange of personnel between the public and private sectors was encouraged and facilitated.

In the view of the American president and British prime minister, the state and the public sector were inefficient, unproductive and extravagant. They extolled market economics and the values and dynamism of the private sector. During their era corporations became the yardstick for economic and social organisation and their values of efficiency, achievement and competition were endorsed. As a result, financial success, individualism and the values of the private sector became dominant in the US, Europe and most countries around the world.

Among the results of these changes during the Thatcher/Major era was the adoption by Britain in January 1996 of the Civil Service Code, updated in 2006. This is a code of conduct setting out the rules of behaviour for civil servants and their role, duties, standards and values, such as probity, trustworthiness, impartiality and objectivity. The code lays down principles such as respect for parliament and the government, nondisclosure of confidential information without prior consent, and non-exploitation of authority for personal objectives. Civil servants are forbidden to express their personal opinions or publish articles in the press on controversial issues.

In France, while there exists no public code of conduct applying to all public employees, there are various rules, regulations and laws setting out their rights and responsibilities in the three public sectors of central government, the provinces and regions, and health. These rules, procedures and laws are sufficient to render a comprehensive code of conduct redundant. France has established committees for proper conduct in these three sectors of the public service.

The French police are the only public administration to have adopted a code of conduct and it is displayed in all French police stations. There is still a prevailing belief in France that a code of conduct is something peculiar to the self-governing professions. The first such code of conduct was the medical one ratified in 1947. Currently, however, there are efforts in France to put in place a code of conduct for the public service with the aim of freeing it from state supervision and allowing it to self-monitor.

In Belgium, Poland, the Czech Republic and Hungary there is no civil service code of conduct. There are however legal provisions covering the rights and duties of public servants just as in France. Both Portugal and Italy have civil service codes of conduct.

The situation in Arab countries resembles to a large extent that in Belgium and France. There is no general code of conduct for public employees, though they exist in some Arab countries for some self-governing professions such as the law, medicine and engineering. For public employees there are rules, regulations and laws setting out in detail their rights and responsibilities, though the names vary from one country to another. For example in the Kingdom of Saudi Arabia the rights and duties of public servants are set out in the Civil Service Law and its implementing regulations. In Kuwait there is the Civil Service Law, in Oman the Administrative Law, in Egypt the Law of Civil Servants, and in Lebanon the Lebanese Regulations for Employees. In the Arab Maghrib there is no general code of conduct other than those for the self-governing professions, although there are rules, regulations and laws setting out the rights and duties of public employees similar to those in France.

Civil service laws in Arab countries recognise two categories of public service, either permanent or temporary. Anyone undertaking permanent work in a public facility so designated by law is deemed a permanent employee, and anyone carrying out a finite task for a specified period is deemed a temporary employee. Such temporary jobs are those with a time limit or particular season, and they end when that period or season ends or when the job itself is completed. These posts are created and vacated according to the organisation's needs and the funds allocated for the job. The rules and procedures applicable to permanent posts in the public service do not apply to temporary posts.

In Europe there are two arrangements for civil service jobs, one of permanent employment and one that involves outsourcing work. In the latter case public service work comes to resemble work in the private sector. The job to be done is quantified and specified in detail and the contractor engaged for that task alone. His contract ends when the job is finished. This arrangement provides no security for the person concerned and provides no security for his future career. Such outsourcing is used in Britain, Sweden, Denmark, Holland and Germany.

Permanent employment is radically at variance with this. Public service positions are defined by their job descriptions, responsibilities, and the conditions to be met by the officials holding them. They are classified into clearly defined groups, which are named, ranked and assessed at their various grades in line with the rules, provisions, terms and procedures laid down by law. Each is placed on a salary scale, and given a job description and a statement of minimum qualifications and skills required, whether academic or practical or both. Everything is protected by law and these employees have a sense of continuity, security and reassurance in their jobs.

Arrangements for permanent public employment in Italy, Greece, France, Spain and Portugal have been influenced by the revolutionary history of those countries. Some have only recently become democracies, and these have enacted laws and regulations to ensure the political neutrality of their public administrations. This has helped to engender continuity and professionalism in the public service.

There is little doubt that the outsourcing option serves the desire to keep civil servants close to the public and civil society, whereas the permanent employment option embodies an explicit ambition to place the public interest first. A mix of the two is perhaps ideal and affords the most beneficial outcome. It appears that this variation in the provision of public services arises from the nature of the state and the extent to which it is federal or centralised. It also seems to depend on the state's understanding of the nature of the public interest, of its role in achieving the objectives of public service, and of the impact of reform and the need to accommodate decentralisation, multiculturalism and the multiplicity of languages in some countries, and to bridge the gap that sometimes occurs between national and local public service.

The proposal that government and public administration should be managed in the same way as private sector companies has an ideological dimension that ignores the purpose and product of the public sector. The objective of companies is to create wealth and profit, whereas fundamental aims of government and the public administration are to foster social and national cohesion, economic growth, security, justice and education.

However there is a problem, and it lies in an ever-decreasing confidence in the public administration, which in turn has a negative impact on the legitimacy of the government and its institutions. This loss of public confidence is fed by scandals caused by the wrongdoing of some public servants, notably a rise in corruption, bribery and fraud in some public departments. Added to this is the misuse of human and technical resources. This is a symptom of the ever-widening gulf between the competitive and dynamic private sector, which exploits information technology to the full, responds rapidly to change, and transfers employees and jobs from one profession to another, and the public sector which operates in its own closed world, with sclerotic bureaucratic procedures and systems for protecting jobs and hidden unemployment.

We must conclude on balance that it is not appropriate for the public sector to go for wholesale adoption of the mechanisms of the private sector. By this we do not mean that the public sector should be allowed to go its own sweet way when it comes to efficiency, but rather that some, but only some, of the techniques of the private sector in administration and employment should be applied to public services. Likewise the management of human resources in the public services must be modernised and improved, up-to-date technologies and especially information technology must be adopted, and corruption must be combated.

The public service ethos

In democratic societies public employees are deemed to be servants of the state deriving their sense of self-worth from doing their public duty. They are people of integrity carrying out their tasks on behalf of the public interest, who are committed to the good reputation of the state to whose service they have dedicated themselves. Public servants should be characterised by altruism and unselfishness, effacing their personal interests in the name of the public good.

Historically public service has been regarded as a noble calling and a patriotic duty. However public administration persists in being inefficient, as is democracy itself, and finds dealing with money a difficult area. It is afraid of human weakness in the face of temptation, and of the power of self-interest over officials and politicians. A code of conduct is an essential safeguard against such lures and against the erosion of democratic values.

The American attitude to the personal interest of public servants differs from that in Europe. In the United States personal interest is acknowledged as the motive for most charitable and humanitarian works, and it is accepted that public servants seek to increase their personal standing. Seeking good repute in this way is not necessarily unethical. In fact it can be the exact opposite, provided always that the public servant maintains his probity and integrity and avoids any conflict of interest.

It is strange that until recently in Western countries the corruption or bribery of a foreign public official was deemed neither unlawful nor disreputable, and went unpunished because no law had been broken. Even now no Western country criminalises the corruption and bribery of foreigners, except for the United States, which has done so only recently. In the West the bribery of a public servant in a foreign country was regarded as a necessary evil even if it was in violation of national laws.

Only since the 1990s have Western countries awoken to the fact that the bribery of employees in the developing world has become costly and damaging to the international economy because it undermines fair competition, holds back social development, dents confidence among investors as well as international and local institutions, demoralises the local public, and exposes the country to risk.

Because its causes are many and complex, there can be no doubt that corruption in its various shapes and forms hinders development and democracy. Its roots are to be found in the history and cultures of peoples and their way of life. Corruption grows when state institutions are weak or have lost their legitimacy, or as a result of disruption caused by national economic policies. The economic impact of corruption is disastrous because funds that otherwise would contribute to growth are embezzled and diverted to personal use, and a weak administration is then unable to fulfil the role entrusted to the civil service. Corruption also leads to a loss of investor confidence and inflates the cost of goods and services. And it fuels the unofficial or black economy. All of this impedes the attainment of targets for sustainable development to such an extent that fighting corruption has become a top priority in some countries.

The sheer scale and complexity of this social and economic evil makes a step-by-step response necessary, starting with limited objectives. The first aim must be to understand the phenomenon of corruption. Before eradicating it, its nature must be understood and its numerous features identified. Only once it has been diagnosed can an appropriate and effective treatment be devised.

The second objective must be to control corruption and place it under surveillance because, while its rapid eradication is impossible, it is possible to rein it in, monitor it and lessen its negative impact in a reasonably short timeframe if a comprehensive approach is taken to fighting it. Here a code of conduct and enforcement of the law play a vital part. There are countries whose anti-corruption legislation is tied in to international law, specifically the Convention Against Corruption ratified by the United Nations on 31 October 2003 and covering money laundering. Other countries have resorted to awareness campaigns under the slogan 'Clean Hands' to promote sound government and transparency. Economic development assistance has been subjected to monitoring and civil society has been enrolled in the fight.

Turning now to public property law, this is designed in principle to prevent public employees availing themselves of public property and services. Public employment law too sets out the terms and obligations preventing the acquisition of public property. Violations of this take the form of theft, deception and fraud, or the use of public service facilities for personal purposes, such as housing, servants, cars, secretaries, communications, office equipment and so on.

Various countries have instituted administrative reforms and introduced new legislation and codes of conduct to serve the public interest, in a quest to restore the good reputation of the civil service and help it to play a more effective role in competition. The aim is also to help public departments adjust to the consequences of globalisation by combating fraud and looking outside their closed worlds, enabling them to compete with the private sector. Examples of these countries are as follows.

The Spanish government enacted a new public employment law on

12 April 2007. This sets out key values for staff in public administration, based on the principle of service to citizens and the paramountcy of the public interest. Those wishing to join the public administration or obtain promotion must subscribe to these values, which include equal treatment, fair entitlement, competence, impartiality, efficiency, transparency, appraisal and responsibility. Articles 52 and 54 of the Spanish law lay down the behaviour required of public servants, listing the professional values needed as respect for equality, loyalty, impartiality, integrity, efficiency and professional confidentiality. They also set out the ethical values required of public employees: consideration, attentiveness, respect and a mild manner towards others, a desire to give the public accurate information, and an obligation to undergo training and propose ways of improving efficiency.

In 2003 the Danish government issued a document enunciating rules for employees. It sets out the code of conduct for public servants and forms part of employment law. The values emphasised are equal treatment, impartiality, flexibility, integrity, respect, professional responsibility and efficiency. The document also deems it a duty of public officials to set citizens an example of proper conduct, to ensure equal treatment and openness, and to inculcate a sense of responsibility and acceptance of reform.

In Canada a code of conduct was adopted for public employment in September 2003. Its aim is to formalise the bonds of trust between the civil service and the public. This code is divided into four categories of values:

1. Democratic values, the object of which is to guide the public administration leadership in serving the public interest in accordance with the law and the constitution.

2. Professional values, requiring public employees to serve citizens to the best of their ability, competently, efficiently, objectively and impartially.

3. Ethical values, requiring work to be performed in a manner that fosters public confidence, the foremost being trustworthiness, fairness, confidentiality, reticence, and sound management of public resources.

4. Social values: respect, courtesy, good working relations with superiors, colleagues and the public, and accountability.

In this way codes of conduct based on moral values have become one of the chief pillars of modernisation and reform in a country such as Canada.

In France the principles on which the French Republic was founded in the 1848 constitution remain the source of values for public employment. These were converted into slogans for the Republic in the 1958 constitution. They are liberty, equality and fraternity, from which flow the principles of continuity, egalitarianism and accommodation to change. These principles inform the public service laws, and are applied to all public service departments; from them are derived the values of impartiality, secularism and equal opportunity. The regulations of 1946 and 1983–84 spelled out the rights and duties of public employment. Some of these legal regulations contain contradictions that are difficult to reconcile. For example public employees must obey their superiors but must also refuse to carry out their orders if they are unlawful. These regulations also confer on employees the right of freedom of opinion and expression, though they are also bound to refrain from expressing their opinions and convictions regarding the service in which they work. Again, while it is their duty to provide the public with information, they also have to maintain professional secrecy and ensure confidentiality.

Unlike other countries in the North, France has only recently begun to consider reform of its public service. This is a result of new attitudes in French society and the impact of private sector values. A number of major corporations have adopted a comprehensive code of conduct setting out their core values. For example the hotel operator ACCOR has adopted one covering renewal, performance, market penetration, respect and confidence, while the bank BNP Paribas has adopted another one, stressing commitment, aspiration, creativity and interaction.

In the public sector each profession has moral and professional responsibilities that have been embodied in regulations, laws or decrees.

For example the values underpinning the work of the public taxation departments are: taxation based on citizenship, professional confidentiality, probity, fair and universal liability to pay taxes, equal opportunity, solidarity, and care for the individual.

In 2007 the Ministry of Economy, Finance and Industry, which includes responsibility for employment, declared its core values to be aptitude for the job, commitment, dedication, loyalty, the art of listening to others, and a spirit of collective endeavour. The French National Audit Office and Ministry of Foreign Affairs set up ethics committees as part of the public service reforms undertaken by them.

In Britain the reform of the public administration started in the Blair era, with the reappraisal of professional and ethical values. In addition to the traditional ones such as integrity, reticence, impartiality, trustworthiness, legality and continuity, in June 2006 the British government added four new values – pride in one's work, commitment, promptness, and professional skill. These were set out in a guide to public administration with a commentary on how they were to be implemented by civil servants. The government also set up a committee of fifteen members whose task would be to monitor adherence to professional values and the ethics of public service.

The Blair government, enthused by the concepts of flexibility, reform and modernisation, developed the New Public Management paradigm, whose declared aim was to shift the consensus away from permanent employment and in favour of outsourcing. The concept of flexibility appeared as a result of political, social and economic changes in Europe and their impact on the needs and challenges facing the public service. During the last twenty years Europe has liberalised its economy, unified its currency, developed its common market and opened up politically towards Eastern Europe. This has led to economic stagnation, a rise in unemployment, social problems and the outbreak of ethnic and nationalist conflicts, which in turn have adversely impacted on community life. At the same time a new economic ideology, namely globalisation, has appeared and extended its reach, with its claims that there is no need for the functions of state and public administration, that public expenditure constitutes a squandering of wealth, and that the public service should enter the arena of the market and competition.

Thus in Britain, under the slogan of flexibility, modernisation and reform of public administration, a new culture has been fostered emphasising competition, contracts, objectives, performance, appraisal and results. Human resources have come to be managed on the principles of decentralising responsibilities and harmonisation with market systems.

The central thrust of the policy of New Public Management was to bring the methods of public service management closer to those of corporate management in the private sector, by downgrading the application of bureaucratic management systems and procedures, harnessing the profit motive, developing commercial-style relationships, and prioritising customer satisfaction in the delivery of public services, treating citizens as consumers rather than as people to be managed.

Consumers are naturally concerned for services to be of as high a quality and as speedy and efficient as possible. This sets the Anglo-Saxon model, the model of absolute liberalisation, apart from the model prevalent in other countries, which does not allow the market free rein but rather seeks to develop what is called a modified market economy that takes into account social cohesion and protection.

The New Public Management approach gave rise to a policy for public administration called 'The Next Step', which introduced the following principles into the public service:

- Division of administrative units
- Competitive tendering
- Personal responsibility for operation and management
- Mechanisms for measuring performance
- Monitoring and control of results
- Management of employees using private sector methods
- Drip-feeding the delivery of resources and services to the consumer, i.e. the public

This reform led to the creation of Next Steps executive agencies charged with the task of implementing the everyday administration arising from contracts negotiated with independent service providers. The implementation of policy remained with the ministry.

In line with the New Public Management reforms a programme was adopted called 'market testing'. Its objective was the ongoing appraisal of public service activities performed by outside contractors, the desire being to establish whether to continue the engagement of outside service providers by means of tenders, or else to completely privatise the public service in question, such as blue-collar manual work for such tasks as the management of parks and gardens and waste disposal. This policy also extended to public bodies whose white-collar staff were responsible for managing social housing, municipal affairs and financial services.

This new liberalisation spread to various northern European countries such as Sweden, Denmark, Finland and Holland, who were persuaded of the virtues of outsourcing. In these countries the old distinctions between the private and public sectors faded away and the public sector adopted the values of individual efficiency, transparency and customer satisfaction.

Arab countries, with a very few exceptions, are mostly hesitant about reform and modernisation. They are reluctant to review public employment policy, to cut red tape and to reduce the hidden unemployment that public bureaucracy harbours. They are slow to clamp down on corruption, and to propagate the values we have been talking about such as integrity, transparency, trustworthiness and dedication. There is little progress with reforms to place people and values first. All these things would strengthen democracy, provide better services and restore citizens' confidence in the public administration.

It is reform such as this that will enable Arab countries to engage with globalisation actively and in full partnership with the rest of the world, to give due consideration to public welfare and concerns, and to engage with the environmental challenges, rapid technological progress and accelerating economic interaction sweeping the globe. The fundamental purpose of reform would be to formulate a new strategy putting sustainable development centre-stage to ensure a better future for coming generations, without neglecting the improvement and development of conditions as they are now.

What, then, do we mean by sustainable development?

5

Sustainable Development

I S SUSTAINABLE DEVELOPMENT a new technical term, a slogan, or a programme for action?

Everyone uses it, often with no clear idea of what it actually means. The state adopts policies based on sustainable development as their guiding principle. Non-governmental organisations never cease clamouring for it to be followed as an approach responsive to trends in civil society. Major corporations in the private sector include special allocations for sustainable development in their programmes and budgets. Even advertising, public relations and travel agencies use it in their promotions and commit to it in their publicity campaigns.

This trendy, widespread advocacy of sustainable development and its promotion by countries, civil society and business, if it shows anything at all, at the very least indicates the hallowed nature of the concept, because it has practically replaced the term "public interest" all over the world. These days we are scarcely able to discuss the public service or public interest without mentioning its new bedfellow, sustainable development.

In a nutshell, sustainable development initiatives can be described as responses to the needs of the present that try to avoid adverse impacts on the ability of future generations to provide for themselves.

On the basis of this definition it does indeed amount to a new way of framing the public interest, even though it has a global rather than national scope. The reasons for the global relevance of the concept are threefold: environmental, social, and politico-economic.

1. First, planet-wide environmental changes pose major threats to humanity: pollution of water and the oceans, climate change, the warming atmosphere, desertification, and loss of habitats leading to shrinking biodiversity.

2. Second, human misery is a global phenomenon. Poverty is persistent and seemingly resistant to cure, while the wealth gap between individuals, classes and countries continues to widen, exacerbating malnutrition, drinking water shortages, endemic diseases, and exclusion from health and education services.

3. Third, sound international governance is lacking. The imbalance in international relations between rich and poor countries leads to inequitable wealth distribution, while organisations working for sustainable development face difficulties due to the lack of a global government able to enforce universal adherence to treaties, conventions and decisions adopted by the international community.

Non-governmental agencies and corporations, who are the new stakeholders in international relations, are demanding the adoption of policies to promote sustainable development in its three aspects – economics, social justice and the environment – as a new approach to remedy the ills afflicting the whole of mankind, on both local and international levels.

This trend undoubtedly shows globalisation in a positive light, in that the awareness of issues affecting all the inhabitants of the Earth is universal, and everybody understands that that there are problems that cannot be remedied merely at local, national and regional levels because they, and their solutions, are global in nature.

The term sustainable development appeared during the 1990s as an alternative to the term development, which was born with the Cold War and died with the collapse of the Berlin Wall in 1989. The dogma of development was linked to the end of colonialism in Asia and Africa during the 1950s and 1960s, after US President Harry Truman demanded, in 1949, that countries that had not gone through an industrial revolution should be assisted. At that time these were referred to as underdeveloped countries. His objective was to steer them away from the Communist camp, and enable them instead to become new markets for American companies.

This concept of growth calls upon poor countries to follow the example of industrial nations in progressing from poverty to a consumer society. In 1960 the American economist W. W. Rostow summarised this as a passage through five stages:

1. The backward traditional society

2. Establishing the pre-conditions necessary for take-off

3. Take-off itself

4. The drive towards maturity

5. The age of high mass consumption

Thus the terms development and economic growth became synonymous, and publicly funded government development aid became a strategic tool in the hands of rich countries to maintain their spheres of influence and open up new markets.

In 1986 the United Nations defined development as a comprehensive economic, social, cultural and political pathway with the object of improving the life of individuals on the basis of their effective and free participation in development and entitlement to a fair share in its benefits.

As material wealth is not on its own an adequate criterion for defining development, in 1990 the United Nations Development Programme put in place an extra indicator for human development which added health and education as vital indices, thus taking into account the extent to which people are able to exercise choice over their lives. It recognises that income alone is inadequate to ensure freedom of choice and personal control over one's destiny.

Between 1990 and 2000, following the collapse of the Soviet Union, public aid for development declined by 30 percent and was transformed from development aid to humanitarian aid in emergencies and disasters, whether natural events such as earthquakes, floods and hurricanes, or man-made ones such as civil wars, disturbances and internal disputes. Indeed an organised campaign began against the provision of publicly funded development aid to foreign governments on the grounds that it encouraged opulence and corruption and failed to lead to development. Its effect was rather to encourage government consumption and dependence upon aid. This fuelled the demand for such aid to be channelled through non-governmental organisations and for the state to embark upon privatisation of the public sector, liberalise towards a market economy, and encourage exports and imports with the aim of participating in globalisation.

This policy had already taken root in 1980 with the decline in prices of raw materials that led to the debt crisis in poor countries. This crisis reached its peak between 1982 and 1992 and led rich countries to change the direction of public development aid to finance what were called 'structural adjustment plans'. The object was to enable poor countries to obtain new finance and loans. However the true purpose behind these structural adjustment plans was to weaken the state, end rule by a single political party, encourage privatisation and the adoption of a market economy, and force the country to join the drive towards globalisation.

In a number of countries the rapid opening-up attendant on these policies led to increased unemployment and poverty, price rises and social unrest.

Sustainable development arose in response, with the aim of humanising a globalisation process that could be vicious in its effects, and bringing it under control. A new environmental vision arose, asserting the need to care for limited and non-renewable resources. It introduced the concept of universality – that we are all in the same boat, and that the behaviour of one of us affects us all.

However the downside is that the West, having become master of the universe, is fundamentally intent on maintaining its highly developed living standards, while development, as it is occurring in the emerging economies of China, India and Brazil, constitutes economic competition. These countries account for a growing consumption of raw materials previously available to the West alone, and their industrial pollution and rapid demographic growth is adding greatly to the damage inflicted on the environment.

Nonetheless sustainable development was transformed into a global strategy in the UN Conference on Environment and Development in Rio de Janeiro in 1992 in which 173 state presidents and governments participated, leading to what is known as Agenda 21, under the title *The Rio Declaration on Environment and Development*. Proposed by Boutros Ghali, the Secretary General of the United Nations at that time, this strategy contained 27 fundamental principles intended to make sustainable development a genuine reality.

These principles included the following:

Principle 1. Human beings are at the centre of concerns for sustainable development. They are entitled to a healthy and productive life in harmony with nature.

Principle 3. The right to development must be fulfilled so as to equitably meet developmental and environmental needs of present and future generations.

Principle 4. In order to achieve sustainable development, environmental protection shall constitute an integral part of the development process and cannot be considered in isolation from it.

Principle 5. All States and all people shall co-operate in the essential task of eradicating poverty as an indispensable requirement for sustainable development, in order to decrease the disparities in standards of living and better meet the needs of the majority of the people of the world.

Agenda 21 specifies the objective of sustainable development as being harmonisation between economic activity, protection of the environment, and social justice. It calls for thinking to be global and action to be local in the pursuit of economic growth, the fight against poverty and inequality in society, and environmental protection.

The fourth component of sustainable development is solidarity between current and future generations, which means reconciling horizontal concerns, i.e. those of spatial extent, with vertical concerns, i.e. those extending through time.

The central question is, to what extent is it possible to reconcile mutually conflicting aims in the context of fragile international governance still lacking in effective institutions to undertake the tasks of control, regulation and supervision. For example, environmental movements focus exclusively on the environmental component of sustainable development, taking action against the factors causing climate change and seeking to maintain biodiversity. They endeavour to combat food insecurity, desertification and the destruction of forests. They advocate minimal exploitation of fossil fuels, encourage renewable energy, oppose pollution, and so on. However these movements fail adequately to acknowledge the economic interests of emerging countries seeking to enjoy the benefits of Western-style progress.

In contrast, international financial organisations like the World Bank and International Monetary Fund encourage developing countries to rely on the strategy of economic growth as the sole means of combating poverty.

Developing countries are urged to encourage foreign companies to invest in their territory to create employment and produce wealth that will enable them to pay off their accumulated debts. This requires the destruction of natural resources, whether for export in their own right, as in the case of forests, or in the search for raw materials such as minerals and oil, and this in turn leads to the spread of desertification, pollution and the depletion of non-renewable resources. As a result future generations are being deprived in advance of benefits from wealth being produced now.

Non-governmental organisations focus their energies on exposing the evils of a globalisation that rampages outside the control of a fragile international order and which is especially damaging in its social impact, leading as it does to a widening chasm in the distribution of wealth, rising unemployment, entrenched poverty and the marginalisation of more and more people.

Hence the role of sustainable development, so the thinking goes, is to reconcile conflicting and divergent interests, and so to operate in the public interest. It is to ensure a means of livelihood enabling everyone to exercise their rights, today, tomorrow, and everywhere. Thus to achieve sustainable development, the first and foremost requirement has to be the establishment of security, stability and freedom of choice to satisfy needs and ensure health and education. It may well be that sustainable development has become a new fashion to which countries, corporations and civil societies can commit themselves. This is actually envisaged in the United Nations Global Compact of 1999, an initiative to encourage businesses worldwide to adopt sustainable and socially responsible policies. Joining this programme requires the participating company to subscribe to a code of conduct, and since 2004 binds it to respect ten principles. These comprise the following:

Human Rights
Businesses should:

Principle 1: Support and respect the protection of internationally proclaimed human rights; and

Principle 2: Make sure that they are not complicit in human rights abuses.

Labour Standards
Businesses should uphold:

Principle 3: The freedom of association and the effective recognition of the right to collective bargaining;

Principle 4: The elimination of all forms of forced and compulsory labour;

Principle 5: The effective abolition of child labour; and

Principle 6: The elimination of discrimination in employment and occupation.

Environment

Businesses should:

Principle 7: Support a precautionary approach to environmental challenges;

Principle 8: Undertake initiatives to promote environmental responsibility; and

Principle 9: Encourage the development and diffusion of environmentally friendly technologies.

Anti-Corruption

Principle 10: Businesses should work against corruption in all its forms, including extortion and bribery.

In brief we might comment that sustainable development, which has come to embrace so many lists of demands, is a very greedy concept. A few examples will suffice, though these are not exhaustive:

1. In the area of the environment:

    • Biodiversity (the protection of forests and other habitats, and the fight against genetic modification)

    • Water (its management, quality and availability)

    • Pollution of fresh water, the sea and the atmosphere

    • Renewable natural resources (wild fauna and flora, and hunting)

    • Fossil raw materials (minerals, oil etc)

    • Waste and its attendant problems

    • Global warming and its causes

    • Desertification arising from the destruction of forests, and land clearance

2. In the area of the economy:

    • Sustainable agriculture

    • Property rights (land tenure and agricultural reform)

- Food security
- International exchange and fair trade
- The provision of power and transportation
- Economic policies
- Intellectual property rights, e.g. copyright and patents

3. In the social area:
- Health (new diseases, access to medicine, domestic and international health policy)
- Nutrition (food security in both quantity and quality)
- Poverty alleviation
- Population (demographics, town planning, the status of women, birth control)
- Urban policy
- Civil and other rights (the right to work, access to education, provision for old age, social organisation, freedom of information, conflict resolution)

This variety and multiplicity makes sustainability difficult to pin down as a concept. It is an approach, culture or attitude of mind rather than a concrete programme for policy-making and action. That is why it sometimes risks being reduced to mere slogans, or being dismissed as an unworldly yearning for pie in the sky.

Sustainable development and globalisation have eroded the power of local economies to develop in isolation from the world. We now live in an interconnected and interwoven world dominated by the financial markets to such an extent that a fluctuation in a currency exchange rate, or a capital movement, or measures taken by banks, have a massive economic impact both locally and nationally, causing fluctuations in the price of national resources, which in turn have knock-on effects on national budgets. The current financial crisis is perhaps the best example of this. These changed circumstances have left economies today at the mercy of the markets, which have weakened the authority of governments and restricted their room for manoeuvre. Their absorption into global mechanisms of exchange means they can no longer rely on fixed, stable exchange rates in their financial and fiscal planning.

The weakness of states in today's world has robbed them of the ability to put in place the policies or medium-term development plans they desire. Some countries are under the supervision of international financial institutions seeking to resolve their accumulated indebtedness and to help them obtain fresh loans. Sometimes the financial institutions impose economic agendas and projects that conflict with the need for sustainable development, and at other times the policies and interests of multinational corporations are given priority over local efforts and needs.

The greatest beneficiaries of the weakening of the state are non-governmental organisations, and this explains the difficult relations between the two sides. This is because NGOs seek in numerous areas to create parallel structures, some of which are perceived to be in competition with the state, as has been happening at the 2006 International Conference on Agrarian Reform and Rural Development (ICARRD) at Porto Alegre in Brazil. Thus the role of civil society has become fundamental, not merely as an expression of democratic values worldwide, but in its capacity to act as a complementary body maintaining the continuity of the work of the state and international organisations.

At the beginning of this century, in a world still rebuilding its structures and making global reforms within the international community, chaos is still the characteristic associated with globalisation, and there are vociferous calls and growing pressures for it to be subjected to laws and made more humane. Non-governmental organisations are playing a positive role in this context, and thanks to their pressures the issue of cancelling developing countries' debts has been placed on the agenda of major international conferences and the United Nations. It is they who should be given the credit for spreading the ideas of sustainable development and fair trade, and for combating the spread of AIDS.

Over the years various NGOs have begun to mature and are transforming themselves into proper professional bodies, in the process adopting and applying the good governance that has taken root in the corporate sphere. However most of them are still at the stage of research, trial and testing, and there are persistent management flaws such as failures to prioritise objectives or to be in the right place at the right time. This remains the case with many NGOs.

There is therefore no escaping the need for regular monitoring and assessment of NGOs' work, whether by their funders or their beneficiaries. To enable their projects to be implemented successfully and efficiently, good governance, sound management, democracy and transparency are essential. However the search for a role for the state vis-à-vis the financial markets, as they are now and as they evolve, may impact negatively on the current high status enjoyed by NGOs. State involvement with its monitoring agencies will inevitably restrict NGOs' freedom of action and may even pull the rug from under the feet of the International Monetary Fund and the World Bank, in revenge for their silence at a time when experts were warning about the reckless dealing of financial institutions who were declaring profits that were probably in fact just liabilities.

Nonetheless the fear of the state playing a monitoring role stems from a lack of desire to see preventive measures imposed to protect the local economy. The next chapter will deal with the new relationship between the state and the economy.

6

The Free Economy: A Passing Crisis or a Step-Change in Human Civilisation?

D ESPITE GLOBAL ECONOMIC GROWTH in 2008 of 3.8 percent thanks to the emerging economies, it was a bad year by any measure. The financial crisis swept away massive banks, and caused a collapse in the value of US real estate. It saw hunger riots in many developing countries, wild swings in the oil price, and intractable unemployment in developed countries, not to mention genocide and war crimes in Darfur, Iraq, Palestine and elsewhere.

There is no doubt that the financial crisis shocked the new US administration into changing course in favour of the pragmatic consolidation of the role of the state centred on increasing rather than reducing taxes. This major transformation in US ideology is not yet fully fledged, but it has made a break with the Reagan model which took root in California in 1970, spreading to federal America in 1979–80 and then to Mrs Thatcher's Britain. The new model calls for an approach involving more taxation, departure from the policy of keeping the US dollar low to encourage exports, reduction in energy consumption and in reliance on Arab oil, and protection of American goods by introducing an effective tariff regime. In the military sphere the new model calls for an end to the war on terrorism in favour of the political resolution of problems, the end of neo-colonialism, and a reordering of US priorities. There is a recognition that the phase of naked individual greed is over and that financial austerity is essential as a way out of the crisis.

This major transformation suggests that the United States, together with the global economy, are at a crossroads of ideology and practice. Before Reagan came to power, and in fact since 1930, the US had invoked the model of a sponsoring state adopted by Franklin Roosevelt and inspired by Keynesian thinking. It envisaged a paternalistic state that relied upon economic growth, the co-operation of the various classes of society, and economic legislation aimed at preserving social harmony. After the Second World War, Europe adopted this model under the name of the welfare state. During the last twenty years the Reagan/Thatcher model, inspired by Milton Friedman, has replaced it and its principles have become indisputably dominant. Doubters, deemed to be either communists or ignoramuses, were cast into outer darkness. The doctrine of Reaganism declared that the economy would function best when there were no restrictions on the free market, and that government interference had an adverse effect on its workings and the standard of living.

According to this theory the market is able to adjust itself of its own accord to correct any imbalance or failure, and government intervention merely accentuates problems through too much bureaucracy. According to Reagan, government is not the solution but rather is itself the problem.

The principles on which this new liberalisation was based may be summarised in five commandments, as follows:

1. That the state should not interfere in the economy but should restrict its role to facilitating a favourable climate for investment.

2. Market freedom should be imposed.

3. Individualism, free of state regulation, should be the chief motivator of those working in the financial system.

4. Freedom of competition should be safeguarded and monopolies prevented.

5. Everything possible should be opened up to free enterprise and commoditisation, including basic utilities, culture, art and literature.

The cultural values of the new liberalisation are: freedom; personal fulfilment in the sense that an individual creates himself by his own efforts; human dignity; consumerism as a way of life; democracy as a political system; religious freedom and the search for truth through rationalism.

This ideology spawned an avalanche of privatisation engulfing state-owned industries and businesses, health and education services, social welfare provision and even prisons.

The Bush administration represented the triumph of such neo-conservative thinking, resulting in the award of contracts to civilian contractors even in core state arenas such as security and defence. In Iraq, for example, there were almost as many civilians employed by private contractors in the service of the US Army as soldiers serving there.

The implementation of this new liberal ideology led to massive profits being made on the stock market, the creation of tens of thousands of millionaires, company heads being awarded salaries and incentives worth millions a year, and legions of people being drawn into the spiral of easy wealth creation – a new generation of so-called Golden Boys. This was aided by low interest rates that fuelled plentiful credit and the devising of new financial instruments, such as those allowing the banks to grant excessive property loans to anyone who wanted one, and enabling them to make loans to institutions in the form of bundles of securities of a new kind. This all took place without proper regulation, and when the real estate loan crisis exploded in July 2007 more than one and a half million American families lost their homes due to the bankruptcy of the investment banks that had hitherto been the backbone of the US economy. Banks were nationalised to prevent their collapse over the real estate loans and the largest insurance company in the world had to be bailed out by tens of billions from the US Treasury.

President George W. Bush, torch-bearer of the free economy and prophet of easy enrichment, had to ask Congress to ratify the expenditure of $700 billion to buy up the debts of the banks and insurance companies to prevent their ruin. This put paid to the theory that the market can correct itself through its own resources. The real estate loans crisis proved that the state, not the market, is the guarantor of citizens' prosperity. It was clear that the market economy had no effective mechanism for self-reform. It needs government regulation and supervision. This is what the US President, Barack Obama, envisaged when he proposed the allocation of $825 billion to revitalise the US economy.

There are those who ascribe direct responsibility for the real estate mortgage crisis to the law passed by President Bush in 2004. This law unleashed abundant credit facilities enabling low-income and middle-class individuals to buy property with no initial deposit and with no checks on their ability to fulfil the responsibilities of property ownership or to pay the instalments on their loans. The result was a sharp rise in the price of real estate. Others consider the separation between company ownership and management to have caused a weakening of control mechanisms and a failure of moral responsibility, and that this encouraged executive directors to indulge their greed and go in for reckless investment. They lent massive sums to people unable to repay their debts. There were also those who believed the American Federal Reserve and other central banks to be at fault, for having allowed excessively low interest rates stimulating borrowing and lending, especially as these central banks had failed to supervise and control the banks to ensure they had adequate financial liquidity.

Adding to this chorus are those who hold the view that financial capitalism had applied the mentality of the casino and the mafia to the management of finance and world economic affairs in general.

The real estate mortgage crisis arose as follows. Initially building firms and banks would attract deposits from savers and then offer them in the form of loans to those wishing to acquire a property. Then, in a quest to increase profits, the banks began to borrow from each other in order to grant more property loans. Some banks then transformed themselves into comprehensive funding institutions for the property sector and they began to attract shareholders.

Seeking yet further profit and funds these institutions contrived a new method involving the aggregation of housing loans into bundles and their sale as securities to other banks and financial investors. Specialist companies were then created to operate this market, so giving the banks courage to increase their borrowing and grant still more housing loans. The result was an exuberant property market and the banks began to recover their loans from the rise in property prices. Then the banks began to lend to borrowers who had no income, gambling on the probability of a continuing rise in property prices. When property prices began to fall in 2006 the loan market collapsed because borrowers were unable to pay their debts, and it became obvious that property prices had been inflated as a result of hyperactive and unrealistic speculation.

The current crisis appears not to be transient like former ones. Rather it marks the start of a new phase, which no one had predicted because of a deluded belief in easy money and an ever-ascending spiral in property prices, and the illusion that nothing could stop it.

The real estate loan crisis is merely a symptom of a larger malaise consisting of three main elements:

1. Easy money. Following the 1987 collapse, an expansionist monetary policy with low interest rates was adopted. Its objective was to prevent a repetition of the crisis, but the result was the opposite of that intended. The abundance of liquidity fuelled bubbles of speculation that began with dotcom businesses and then moved smoothly on to property, with nothing to stop it.

2. A disregard of risk because of lack of regulation or supervision. The system of intermediaries between the ultimate distributors of the credit (the lenders) and beneficiaries (the borrowers), especially in real estate, grew up in such a way that the distributors were no longer exposed to risk.

3. Neglect of regulation and financial controls. In view of supervision

and accounting deficiencies and a failure of moral responsibility, the market began to act as if governed by the rules of poker. It became possible for someone to sell imaginary properties or ones they did not own and to buy shares without paying for them, all without incurring any liability.

The whole system depended on a continuing rise in share prices and this is at the heart of the current crisis. The unleashing of rampant greed arose from a disregard for moral obligations and inadequate basic rules for the banking profession. Hence today we are facing a crisis that differs from the 1929 crash, because the absorption of losses will take some time, and because we are paying the price for an era of indebtedness during which growth was financed by borrowing unrelated to any realistic prediction of property prices, such that the debts bore no relation to the real economy.

The new order requires the United States to put in place controls that combine adequate protection of institutions with continued stimuli for enterprise and exports to the emerging countries. It is the central banks' responsibility to establish legal controls over the free market. It is the job of the state to lay down sound conditions for economic growth and to supervise and intervene to protect it, and to compel the banks and financial institutions to abide by their moral obligations. It has become apparent that it is the state's abdication of this role that has led to catastrophe. It is essential therefore to have strict supervision conducted by the state. It is also possible, even necessary, for the state to harmonise the driving forces of competition and individual initiative with the requirements of social welfare. This may lead to a revival of Keynesianism, which fell out of fashion in the early 1970s only to be replaced by Reaganomics.

Despite plans and programmes being implemented to rescue financial institutions, the world economy may fall prey to depression if these plans do not also succeed in restoring investor confidence in their positive effects and if depositors are not totally convinced of the security of their deposits. The measures taken by the US and other industrialised countries rely fundamentally on pumping liquidity into the markets, supporting financial institutions facing bankruptcy, guaranteeing deposits and savings, and taking other co-ordinated action to counter the repercussions of the crisis alongside measures to revitalise the economy.

As the US economy constitutes 40 percent of the global economy, the current crisis has damaged all countries. Action is therefore vital to create a unified global banking legislative and supervisory entity with all regional blocs and economic communities participating in its management and subscribing to its policies. It is also crucial to reform the International Monetary Fund and World Bank, the twins that were born in 1944 in Bretton Woods, near Washington, to rescue Europe. They are now living in the past and take action only to intervene in the Third World. However true it may be that these two institutions have evolved since that time, capitalism has transmogrified even more rapidly, to the extent that the International Monetary Fund today controls financial liquidity of less than 1.8 percent of global income. Furthermore the volume of lending by these two twins is extremely low. The real heavy lifting of finance and trade in the world today is done by the largest 200 multinational corporations. These are subject to no regulation or supervision by anyone, in complete contrast to the situation when the IMF and World Bank were founded. When Keynes first proposed the formation of an international monetary fund it was to have resources equal to half of world income, giving it very powerful global financial leverage. However the IMF and the World Bank, founded to provide short-term and long-term lending respectively, have been transformed into mere policemen of capital operations within the Third World, Eastern Europe and Russia.

The Bretton Woods twins are therefore quite unequipped to resolve the problems of capitalism in a financial and economic crisis running out of control. The profits of the financial sector rely on borrowing and lending without end to governments, businesses and households. It is a sector that has grown more and faster than the real economy of national and international trade and production. How can we hope in such circumstances for a stable, efficient international financial system when we have a marginalised international bank and international monetary fund?

The question is whether or not the achievement of stability or a new financial order is in accord with the current financial interests of corporations or with economic liberalisation when there is an economic war, fierce competition and speculations that have led to financial excess and depravity. The Bush administration bears a measure of responsibility for its eagerness to curtail the role of the state in the economy and rely on uncontrolled market mechanisms, and for the colossal US budget deficit that on his watch ballooned to a trillion dollars, even though there was no budget deficit at all when he took office in 2001.

However the United States, despite its massive indebtedness, is not in danger of insolvency. That is due to the unique status of the US dollar, which has not been supported by gold since 1971. Furthermore it has been able to weave a web of international interdependency which is difficult to unravel. The dollar now accounts for the greatest portion of central bank reserves in countries such as China, Japan and Russia, who thus have no interest whatsoever in its collapse or in US bankruptcy. The purchase of US treasury bonds is guaranteed by the massive wealth in the Cayman Islands, the Virgin Islands, Bermuda, China and Japan, and the latter two provide loans and buy US treasury bonds to enable them to sell their commodities into the US market.

Despite the benefits of the dollar's distinctive status, the shock of the current crisis has driven Obama and the US to abandon previous neoliberal dogma and to reassert the role of the state by accepting the idea of increasing taxation. The US also lends its approval to radical measures to overhaul global finance to counter the monetary crisis that has afflicted the banking system all over the world. Such a project can work only if all those responsible for national economic policies in all countries of the world agree to act together to entrench the concept of global governance and moral obligation. They must all accept the necessity for their institutions to be governed by a visionary policy to inject their national economic plans and programmes with strong and appropriate methods for confronting the crisis and finding a way out of it.

The first Arab Economic Summit took place in Kuwait on 19 and 20 January 2009. For more than twenty years the Arab banking system has customarily accepted instructions from the Basel Committee on Banking Supervision and implemented them, most recently Basel II or the second Basel Accords, without the Arabs themselves being represented on the Committee. However, following the Kuwait Summit they now have a responsibility to act by demanding a role for the Arab bloc in the formulation of the Committee's decisions, and indeed of any reform or new rules for the global financial system. The resolution of the Arab Summit to create an Arab Common Market by 2015 undoubtedly indicates a new seriousness of purpose and a commitment to common Arab action, especially as Arab governments broadly agree on the concepts governing economic processes.

This resolution demands a continuation of structural reforms, improved management of investment and development, and the elimination of bureaucratic impediments to the free and secure transfer of Arab capital funds. Naturally there has to be a comprehensive review of investment arrangements and the removal of obstacles to setting up joint Arab projects as a first step towards building an Arab Common Market and integrating Arab economies, especially as the components for integration exist.

Progress towards an Arab Common Market necessitates involving the private sector in this important process, by means of common Arab legislation encouraging it to respond with confidence, and to take up its role in managing the mechanisms of inter-Arab commerce and providing preferential benefits for joint investments. This will depend on essential changes being made in the Arab banking and monetary systems to enable them to participate in financing development and creating infrastructures capable of handling up-to-date, competitive methods of production and export. In an age of large economic blocs an Arab Common Market is vital to confront and contain the repercussions of the global financial crisis, especially as the Arab world suffers from unemployment and external debt, lacks self-sufficiency in food and an advanced technical base, and finds itself unable to attract capable Arab scientific staff.

Citizens in both the Arab East and the Arab West have the right to enjoy freedom of movement and residence, freedom of work and investment, free transfer of capital, freedom of exchange of goods and services, freedom to travel and use transportation facilities, and free and safe entry and exit by seaports, airports and land crossings, just as European citizens and investors do in the European common market.

Conclusion

IN THE FIRST OF THE SIX chapters of this book we examined the collective memory of the Arabs. These narratives have helped to create two distinct and contradictory Arab identities. There are those who see the positive features of the Arab cultural past, with its vision of intellectual openness, toleration and exchange. Those adopting this approach believe that the dynamic values underpinning the splendours of Arab civilisation are the very same as the ones informing current Western progress, even though they have been given modern expression and new formulations and go by different names.

The opposing tendency believes that the West represents the antithesis of Arab culture and that every feature shared with the West means a dilution of Arabness. This mindset is derived from a closed, puritanical view of culture and identity, which cannot countenance the existence of features, however limited, that are shared with outsiders and are a result of cultural interaction throughout history.

This tendency fears the power of the other to undermine it, stresses the importance of opposing it as the only means of preserving itself, and is consumed with hatred for it. As this mentality is based not on confidence, but on fear, it suffers from a deep sense of isolation and rejection. It blames this on the opposing camp, and so imagines it has no option but to spurn it and wall itself off from it.

This negative view of history leads to outmoded interpretations. Its proponents become so obsessed with the past that they mythologise it, ascribing to it high ideals that transcend the actual reality. The superiority of the positive view infects those with this nostalgic vision of civilisation with pessimism, self-flagellation, an abhorrence of their present predicament, and a tendency toward suicidal violence. Figuratively speaking, they are lamenting over an abandoned encampment, a frequent trope in ancient Arab poetry.

As against this we can identify in the West a tendency towards an over-simplification of history that places Greek philosophy and European rationalism on a pedestal and so plays down the prior rationalist currents in China, India and ancient Egypt as well as subsequent Islamic and Arab rationalism and philosophy. This extreme tendency, subscribed to by some in the West, has led to violence and domination, and a desire to impose its 'civilising mission' through colonialism, occupation and ideas of racial supremacy, as well as conservatism in contemporary Western cultures.

In Chapter 2 we dealt with the debate on globalisation vis-à-vis the nation state. In it we attempted to lay a foundation for discussion of globalisation's economic, educational and cultural impacts and the risks of global terror, and asked whether or not globalisation constitutes an opportunity for genuine Arab revival, and how this might be achieved.

Chapter 3 addressed the question of moral responsibilities and their influence on productivity, employee morale and the establishment of modern state institutions. We also set out the human and professional values needed for reform and development, and the importance of respecting the rights of white- and blue-collar workers.

Chapter 4 presented a discussion of sound governance and administrative reform of the public sector in various countries, and dealt with the moral obligations of companies and the phenomenon of corruption in its various shapes and forms. We noted how the absence of regulation has led to abuse and contributed to the creation of the current financial crisis, and how this necessitates controls being placed on the global banking and monetary system, and calls for funds to be made available to stimulate economic growth to seek a way out of the crisis.

It was necessary next to devote a whole chapter to defining the various concepts of sustainable development and examining them in their historical, political, environmental and socio-economic framework. We spoke of the dangers threatening the planet and the human misery caused by persistent and intractable poverty, and by the lack of sound international governance to correct imbalances between rich and poor countries and to eliminate injustice in international relations.

Chapter 6 summarises and discusses neo-liberalism and the free-market economy, the role of the state, and the financial crisis with its subsequent disasters. It calls upon the West to review all its options and its way of life, and especially its modes of production. It then calls for structural resolutions of the current crisis to be considered, by which we mean the negative effects of globalisation. It is true that global investment had been beneficial during times of economic prosperity. However it can be extremely detrimental at times of crisis, especially in developing countries not in a position to demand social and economic guarantees to accompany global investments, and having no legislation for the regulation and supervision of foreign investments.

The escalation of the economic crisis and the severe collapse of confidence among consumers and investors that attended it, along with the reduction in expenditure in every part of the world, have deprived the economy of its fuel and led to depression and a severe reduction in growth rates. Some sectors have even undergone recession, such as car manufacture, power generation and insurance. Various governments have allocated hundreds of billions of dollars to plans to revive the economy. However they have confined the benefit from these funds exclusively within their own countries. This has led to the closure of company branches around the world and a halt to work in their factories in developing countries, including the Arab world. For example, the tourism and travel industry saw a reduction in its share of annual gross domestic product of 12 percent during 2009–10, according to the World Tourism and Travel Council.

Studies by the WTTC and Oxford Economics show the current slump in the tourism and travel industry to have been sudden, with no prior warning signs and no indication of an early upturn. Some people regard China and the other emerging countries as the best prospective driving force for growth in tourism, especially in the light of studies showing that China itself will provide about 100 million international tourists. China in practical terms is the only country that has adopted a plan for economic revival. It is valued at 461 billion euros, that is 13 percent of annual domestic product. Its aim is to invest to achieve a qualitative change in the Chinese model, by which it means reform of the social and economic infrastructure, by concentrating on human capital, technological innovation and the green economy in order to restore an economic balance in favour of consumption.

China understood early on that the shortage of raw materials and energy could be remedied only by new economic planning. The question is to what extent China, in seeking to deal with it, has understood that the current crisis has made the export-based development model a thing of the past.

Economists in America anticipate three scenarios for an emergence from crisis and a return to economic growth. The first one predicts that the depression will persist for a long time and that any return to growth will be much weaker than expected. This analysis has been adopted by Sung Won Sohn, a professor at the University of California. However Stephen Roach, director of the Morgan Stanley bank in Asia, considers that the return to economic growth will be tortuous, with short-lived fluctuations. Thirdly, Nouriel Roubini forecasts that the recession will persist for the foreseeable future and that there will never be any real return to the economic growth of the past.

In commenting on the crisis Michael Spence, a professor at Stanford University and holder of the 2001 Nobel Prize for economics, stated his belief that the downward spiral of recession has in fact occurred because of interactions within the global economy, and that any remedy for the crisis will depend greatly on the ability of governments to co-ordinate their policies and take collective decisions to intervene to revive the real economy and regulate and control the financial economy. If governments do manage to co-ordinate their intervention, we shall see light at the end of the tunnel in 2010, otherwise the situation will deteriorate further.

We deduce from this divergence of opinion that no one knows precisely when or how we shall escape from the current unprecedented crisis. A restoration of public trust in corporate chiefs and management is not guaranteed. There must be an overhaul of corporate governance, management and policies. But even then how are investor and consumer confidence to be restored? This issue also includes the personal factor, especially if there is no clear and convincing plan of escape from the crisis that will raise the level of public faith in leaders and officials.

Will the results of the London G20 summit in April 2009 contribute to a restoration of this confidence as the participants hope and expect? (See Appendix 2.)

The formation of the G20 has led to a weakening of the G8, the nations of which have gradually slipped from their previous global economic hegemony. Since the financial crisis began in September 2008 the intervention of the G8 (the seven major industrialised countries plus Russia) has been restricted to the issue of communiqués and preliminary positions that have left the actual decisions to the G20.

The G7 group of major industrialised countries was formed informally in 1975 as a club with the aim of ordering and furthering international economic and political priorities. Russia subsequently joined this club in the vanguard of the global economy, and it became the G8. However today it is no longer possible for this group to take the lead in numerous fields, such as the environment or financial and commercial issues, without the approval of China, India, Brazil and South Africa, which are member countries of the G20. How for example would it be possible to undertake reform of the financial system without involving China, which holds the largest currency reserves in the world?

At a meeting of its leaders in L'Aquila, Italy, during 8–10 July 2009, the G8 undertook to provide $12 billion for food security in the hope that this would play a crucial role in determining the priorities and direction of the G20 at its second meeting in Pittsburgh in the United States on 24–25 September 2009, and it was decided that this meeting would be dedicated to the reform of the global monetary system.

There is no denying the fundamental contradiction between the G8 retaining its lead responsibility for major issues around the world, and the G20, which seeks to supersede this small group of countries. The G20 has usurped the role of the United Nations and its specialist agencies, and has taken upon itself the responsibility for major issues around the world.

Finally when will the recommendations and resolutions of the G20 lead both to a balanced, transparent implementation that is equitable to all parties and a new and more stable basis for breathing new life into the world economy?

Furthermore there are reservations regarding the G20, because the major industrialised countries still retain a greater influence within it than they should, and the emerging countries are lobbying for reforms to ensure their voice is heard. The latter, consisting of Brazil, Russia, India and China and known as the BRIC Group, refuses to remain on the sidelines. So there is a possibility that these considerable tensions between the emerging and industrialised countries may cause them to abandon their current efforts to adopt unified positions on international problems arising from the global financial crisis.

Any attempt to settle issues related to the environment, society, employment, transparency, corruption in international relations, money laundering, financial safe havens and so on, if it is defective, will fail to produce the desired stability, put the current crisis behind us, or improve our political and economic prospects.

The London G20 summit proclaimed the birth of a new world that is less neo-liberal and Anglo-Saxon and more balanced economically and politically. The free-market economy that regards everything as a commodity to be bought and sold is no longer triumphant. The summit sentenced the free-market economy to regulation and control – in other words, the liberalisation promulgated by Reagan and Thatcher has come to an end. All talk today is of a capitalism in need of a strong state able to control it with financial and legal regulations, with no exceptions for tax havens. Also among the features of the summit was open discussion of the need to end the sole authority of the US dollar as a global reserve currency. The euro, the Japanese yen and the Chinese yuan are challenging the dollar's supremacy. They are seeking an equal role in global exchange through the International Monetary Fund, and are demanding a new currency as reference point for all currencies in the world.

Surely the results of the G20 and G8 summits present a golden opportunity for Arab countries to implement the resolutions of the Kuwait Economic Summit (see Appendix 1) and unite Arab countries with a modern infrastructure, facilitating the movement of goods and people and so contributing to the creation of job opportunities for millions and an Arab Common Market that will help counter the current crisis.

Yes, the Arabs can too! They are quite capable of redoubling their efforts at both public and private level to achieve Arab economic and social integration and development, making them better able to participate in the global economy, to negotiate with regional and international political and economic blocs, and to confront the repercussions of the global financial crisis on Arab countries and peoples.

Yes. There is sufficient official and popular Arab awareness to engender a new dynamism – a force that will reclaim a proper, effective role for the Arab nation in the great project to build contemporary human civilisation, and to ensure a better future for Arabs today and generations to come.

APPENDICES

Appendix 1

Resolutions issued by the Arab Economic, Development and Social Summit held in Kuwait, 19-20 January 2009

The Global Financial Crisis and its Impact on Arab Economies

The Council of the Arab League at Summit level has studied the following:

- The memorandum of the Secretariat General
- The report of the Secretary General to the Arab Economic, Development and Social Summit
- The resolution of the Economic and Social Council passed at its Extraordinary Session, no. Q-1756 D.Gh.A, dated 4/12/2008
- The Arab Monetary Fund study entitled *The International Financial Crisis and its Repercussions on Arab Economies*
- The study of the Organisation of the Arab Petroleum Exporting Countries (OPEC)
- The results of the meeting between Arab Ministers of Finance, Governors of the Central Banks and Arab Monetary Institutions, and the Heads of the Arab Finance Funds, to study the repercussions of the global financial crisis on Arab economies, held in Kuwait on 14/1/2009

The Council resolves:

1. To insist on continuing support by Arab countries of their national financial institutions and strengthening of their monitoring and supervision.
2. That Arab countries should play a more effective role in international economic relationships and participate in international efforts to ensure world financial stability.
3. That the Governors of the Central Banks and Arab Monetary Institutions should increase co-ordination and liaison between the supervisory organisations in Arab countries.
4. To insist on the continued provision of support for Arab financial institutions to enable them to play an effective role in increasing Arab cash flows and mutual Arab investments, and in particular integrated Arab projects, and to assist Arab countries in their efforts to improve the investment climate.
5. To make the arrangements necessary for Arab financial institutions to anticipate any future adverse impacts of the global financial crisis on Arab economies and provide alternative methods of coping with this.
6. To insist on the importance of stability in oil prices in global markets out of regard for the economic interests of producers and consumers.
7. To increase co-ordination between the ministers of finance in Arab countries and instruct them to study the best methods for this.

Q.Q:3D.A(1)-J4, dated 20/1/2009

Arab Electricity Linkage Projects

The Council of the League at the Summit level has studied the following:

- The memorandum of the Secretariat General
- The report of the Secretary General to the Arab Economic, Development and Social Summit
- The paper for the project "To enhance Arab electricity linkage projects" presented by the Executive Office of the Council of Arab Ministers concerned with electricity affairs
- The report and resolutions of the Economic and Social Council at its Extraordinary Session held on 2–4 December 2008

– It takes cognizance of the resolutions of the successive Arab Summits in this regard: Resolution 212, Paragraph 3, issued by the 13th Summit held in

Amman in 2001; Resolution 236 issued by the 14th Summit held in Beirut in 2002; Resolution 311 issued by the 17th Arab Summit held in Algiers in 2005.

– It affirms the importance of Resolution 399 issued by the 19th Arab Summit held in Riyadh in 2007 regarding the implementation of the study "A comprehensive Arab electricity link and assessment of the exploitation of natural gas for the exportation of electricity" and its role in establishing an Arab market for electricity.

The Council resolves:

1. To hasten to complete the Arab electricity linkage projects in accordance with the project document "To enhance Arab electricity linkage projects" and act to complete the remaining steps in accordance with the priorities to be decided by the Arab Council of Ministers concerned with electricity affairs.
2. That Arab countries should take the steps necessary to implement Arab electricity linkage projects without impediments, including the amendments, adjustments, and updating of national legislation and related regulatory frameworks.
3. To request the Arab Fund for Economic and Social Development to continue to provide the finance necessary for the execution of Arab electricity linkage projects and establish a mechanism for the financing of the execution of these projects on a commercial basis with the participation of the private sector, and affirm the importance of the role of the private sector in the transfer and establishment of modern technology within the Arab nation.
4. To include the private sector in the projects related to the formation of an Arab market for electricity.
5. To instruct the Arab Council of Ministers concerned with electricity affairs in co-operation with the Arab Fund for Economic and Social Development to draw up a timetable and mechanism for implementation to complete the Arab electricity linkage projects and prepare periodic reports for the Summit on the progress achieved in this respect.

Q.Q:4D.A(1)-J4, dated 20/1/2009

Plan for an Arab Railway Link

The Council of the League at Summit level has studied the following:

• The memorandum of the Secretariat General
• The report of the Secretary General to the Arab Economic, Development and Social Summit
• The plan for the Arab railway link that was approved by the Council of Arab Ministers of Transport in its Resolution 308 issued in its Session 21 on 29/10/2008
• The report and decisions of the Economic and Social Council at its Extraordinary Session held on 2–4 December 2008

–The Council takes cognizance of the successive decisions of the Arab Summit regarding enhancing the Arab transportation sector and strengthening the Arab land, sea and air network.

– It takes cognizance of the two regional agreements ratified within the framework of the United Nations Economic and Social Commission for West Asia regarding international roads and railways in the Arab East, together with the programmes and projects in these two areas that were agreed upon within the framework of the Arab Maghrib Union.

– Aware of the importance of linking Arab countries by comprehensive infrastructure networks necessary to facilitate Arab economic integration,

– In the context of a comprehensive strategic vision for the development of the Arab transportation sector in its various forms by land, sea and air,

– In view of the definite benefits of railways regarding the cost of transportation, safety and low energy usage,

– It thanks the Arab Economic and Social Development Fund for its undertaking to finance a comprehensive technical and economic study of the plan.

The Council resolves:

1. To launch the project for an Arab railway link in line with the plan approved by the Council of Arab Ministers of Transport, and that the member countries should take the steps necessary to amend and adjust national legislation and the related regulatory frameworks so that the projects in the

plan can be executed without obstacles.

2. To establish a mechanism for the financing of the execution of these projects on a commercial basis in which participation will be open to the private sector, Arab finance institutions and Arab regional and international finance funds, and that the private sector will be invited to invest in the execution and operation of these projects.

3. That Arab, regional and international finance institutions will be requested to participate in the funding of the execution of these projects.

4. That the Council of Arab Ministers of Transport be instructed to follow up the execution of the projects in the plan for the Arab railway link and the necessary preparation of an agreement for this purpose and present to the Summit periodic reports on the progress achieved in implementation.

Q.Q:5D.A(1)-J4, dated 20/1/2009

The Emergency Plan for Arab Food Security

The Council of the League at Summit level has studied the following:

• The memorandum of the Secretariat General
• The report of the Secretary General to the Arab Economic, Development and Social Summit
• The Arab strategy for sustainable agricultural development ratified by the Riyadh Summit in 2007
• The Riyadh Declaration of 2008 for the enhancement of Arab co-operation to meet the international food crisis
• The plan for the Emergency Arab Food Security Programme Project of 2008 submitted by the Arab Agricultural Development Organisation and approved by the General Assembly of the Arab Agricultural Development Organisation in Session 30, Resolution 23 dated 30/4/2008
• The declaration of the high-level conference of the United Nations Food and Agriculture Organisation concerned with global food security and the challenges presented by climate change and bioenergy, Rome, 5/6/2008
• The report and resolutions of the Economic and Social Council at its Extraordinary Session held on 2–4 December 2008

– In awareness that the state of instability in international food commodity markets, their fluctuating prices and increased use of food crops by a number of advanced countries to produce biofuels, which expose the Arab region to risk and has repercussions on Arab food security in both the short and long term, and especially in the context of an increasing Arab food gap and limited investment in comprehensive Arab agricultural projects,

– In belief in the potential of the Arab region to be self-reliant in the production of the greater part of its food requirements, and to provide and make available adequate food supplies to Arab peoples, especially of basic food commodities,

– With an obligation to achieve Arab food security as a permanent national and Arab policy to achieve Arab national security,

– The Council welcomes the proposal of the United Nations Food and Agriculture Organisation to hold an international conference of heads of state and governments during 2009 regarding the control of international food security.

The Council resolves:

1. To launch the Arab emergency food security programme.
2. To instruct governments of Arab countries that benefit from the components of the programme to grant special preferential benefits for investment in the fields specified in the programme.
3. To request Arab, regional and international development funds to contribute to the provision of the necessary financial requirements for execution of the programme.
4. To invite the private sector to invest in the execution of the programme.
5. To instruct the Arab Agricultural Development Organisation to follow up the implementation in co-ordination with all parties concerned, and provide the Summit with periodic reports regarding the progress achieved.

Q.Q:6D.A(1)-J4, dated 20/1/2009

The Customs Union

The Council of the League at Summit level has studied the following:

• The memorandum of the Secretariat General
• The report of the Secretary General to the Arab Economic, Development and Social Summit
• The report and resolutions of the Economic and Social Council at its Extraordinary Session held on 2–4 December 2008

– The Council takes cognizance of the previous resolutions regarding the formation of the Arab Customs Union, the last of which was Resolution 392 of the Riyadh Summit of 2007 approving the general structure of the Executive Programme for the Arab Customs Union.

– With an obligation to remove all non-customs restrictions, duties and taxes of similar effect that hinder the implementation of the Greater Arab Free Trade Area,

– In affirmation of the desire of the Arab Economic and Social Development Summit to start to take practical steps towards the formation of the Arab Customs Union to achieve an Arab Common Market,

The Council resolves:

1. To conclude all the requirements for the formation of the Arab Customs Union with full implementation of it in 2015, and for the countries that qualify to take the legal measures necessary in preparation for the achievement of the Arab Common Market.
2. To instruct the Economic and Social Council to complete all the measures necessary for this purpose in accordance with the timescales specified in the work programme for the formation of the Arab Customs Union.
3. The Economic and Social Council will submit to the Summit periodic reports on the progress achieved.

Q.Q:7D.A(1)-J4, dated 20/1/2009

Arab Water Security

The Council of the League at Summit level has studied the following:

• The memorandum of the Secretariat General
• The report of the Secretary General to the Arab Economic, Development and Social Summit
• The report of the General Assembly of the Arab Centre for Studies of Arid Zones and Dry Lands (ACSAD) in Session 29, no. 9, on 21–22 May 2008, that adopted the project plan for the comprehensive management of water resources to achieve sustainable development in the Arab region presented by the Arab Centre for Studies of Arid Zones and Dry Lands (ACSAD)
• The report and resolutions of the Economic and Social Council at its Extraordinary Session held on 2–4 December 2008

– It takes cognizance that the Arab region contains 5 percent of the world's population but only 1 percent of the world's water resources, and that 60 percent of the water resources in the Arab region come from outside the region, making the Arab region among the poorest regions of the world in terms of water resources, leading to challenges that impact on Arab national security.

– Within the context of the challenges imposed by climate change and an increase in temperature of the planet, and the adverse effects that will result from this on limited water resources in the Arab nation that suffer from a shortage that it is anticipated will increase in the future, together with the political, economic and social consequences that may arise from this,

– In the belief in the importance of adopting a comprehensive programme for the management of water resources and increasing the efficiency of water use in the Arab region, and of embedding appropriate technologies for the management of these resources, and in recognition of the need for an expansion in the use of non-traditional water resources,

The Council resolves:

1. To instruct the Arab Ministerial Council for Water to draw up a strategy for water security in the Arab region to meet the challenges and future requirements for sustainable development.
2. To approve a project for the comprehensive management of water resources to achieve sustainable development in the Arab region.
3. To invite Arab funds and financial institutions to contribute to the financing of the execution of the project.
4. To instruct the Arab Ministerial Council for Water to co-operate with the Arab Centre for Studies of Arid Zones and Dry Lands (ACSAD) in following up the execution of the project in co-operation with the relevant national institutions in Arab countries.
5. That the Ministerial Council for Water should present periodic reports to the Summit on the progress achieved in execution of the resolution.

Q.Q:8D.A(1)-J4, dated 20/1/2009

Appendix 1

The Comprehensive Programme to Support Employment and Eliminate Unemployment in Arab Countries

The Council of the League at Summit level has studied the following:

• The memorandum of the Secretariat General
• The report of the Secretary General to the Arab Economic, Development and Social Summit
• The resolution of the Arab Labour Conference no. 1369 dated 1/3/2008
• The plan of the Comprehensive Programme to Support Employment and Eliminate Unemployment in Arab Countries
• The report and resolutions of the Economic and Social Council at its Extraordinary Session held on 2–4 December 2008
• The results of the Arab Forum on Development and Employment held in Doha on 15–16/11/2008 and the Doha Declaration issued by it

– The Council asserts that work is a human value and part of civilisation and that work is both a right and duty that must be provided adequately and justly.

– The Council asserts anew that productive employment is one of the most important aspects of development.

– The Council notes that unemployment has become a common phenomenon that threatens social peace.

The Council resolves:

1. To implement a comprehensive programme to support employment and eliminate unemployment in Arab countries through the Arab Labour Organisation and its existing agencies and relevant parties in Arab countries.
2. To adopt the period from 2010 to 2020 as an Arab decade for employment and reduce unemployment to a half by the beginning of 2020; to give priority in development policies in Arab countries to support effective and productive employment and create job opportunities, eliminate unemployment, improve living standards and the work conditions of employed people.
3. To concentrate national and Arab efforts on supporting human development and effective training that meets the requirements of the labour market and raises the productive competence of Arab workers, and to seek to develop three of the existing training centres in Arab countries.
4. That the governments of Arab countries should take the measures necessary to facilitate the movement of the Arab workforce between its member

countries in accordance with their requirements.

5. To support initiatives of the private sector and Arab finance institutions and funds to implement the programme and reduce the rates of unemployment at both the national and Arab level.

6. To instruct the Arab Labour Organisation and Secretariat General of the League to provide periodic reports to the Summit on the progress achieved.

Q.Q:9D.A(1)-J4, dated 20/1/2009

The Arab Programme to Eliminate Poverty in Arab Countries

The Council of the League at Summit level has studied the following:

• The memorandum of the Secretariat General
• The report of the Secretary General to the Arab Economic, Development and Social Summit
• The Arab programme to execute the Arab strategy to eliminate poverty in Arab countries
• The report and resolutions of the Economic and Social Council at its Extraordinary Session held on 2–4 December 2008

– The Council confirms all its resolutions related to policies to reduce poverty in the Arab nation including the resolution of the Beirut Summit D.A(14) no. 240, dated 28/3/2002, regarding the remedy for poverty in the Arab nation.

– The Council applauds the achievement of Arab countries in the field of reducing poverty.

– Desiring to improve the standard of living and increase the prosperity of citizens of Arab countries,

– The Council affirms anew the determination of Arab leaders to achieve social progress and eliminate the phenomena of marginalisation and isolation and preserve the cohesion of the social fabric in Arab societies.

– It affirms the importance of continuing the programme related to policies for the reduction of poverty and the provision of the necessary finance for social security networks.

– It emphasises the obligation to achieve the development and objectives for the millennium and enhance their progress in accordance with the resolution of the General Assembly of the United Nations no. 55/2 dated 8/9/2000.

The Council resolves:

1. To implement the Arab programme to eliminate poverty in Arab countries within a period of four years and finance the programme's projects, and invites Arab finance institutions to participate in funding it.
2. To put in place socio-economic policies that will lead to a reduction in the rate of poverty by a half by 2015 at the latest.
3. To undertake to finance social security networks and provide the finance necessary for small and medium-sized projects.
4. To instruct the Council of Arab Social Affairs Ministers to follow up the implementation of the programme and present a report to the Summit on the progress achieved in this regard.

Q.Q:10D.A(1)-J4, dated 20/1/2009

The Arab Programme for the Implementation of the Developmental Objectives for the Millennium

The Council of the League at Summit level has studied the following:

• The memorandum of the Secretariat General
• The report of the Secretary General to the Arab Economic, Development and Social Summit
• The Arab Programme for the Implementation of the Developmental Objectives for the Millennium in the Least Developed Arab Countries
• The report and resolutions of the Economic and Social Council at its Extraordinary Session held on 2–4 December 2008

– The Council confirms all its previous resolutions, the last of which was the Resolution of the Khartoum Summit, D.A (18), no. 356, dated 29/3/2006, regarding the Arab Declaration on the Developmental Objectives for the Millennium.

– It affirms the extreme importance of the success and sustainability of the human development programme to widen people's options.

– It affirms the undertaking to achieve the developmental objectives for the millennium and enhance their progress in accordance with the resolution of the General Assembly of the United Nations no. 55/2 dated 8/9/2000.

The Council resolves:

1. To implement the Arab declaration to achieve the developmental objectives of the millennium during the period 2009–10, concentrating on the least developed Arab countries.
2. That the least developed Arab countries shall present an annual report to the League General Secretariat regarding the progress they have achieved in implementing the developmental objectives for the millennium. It will specify the aid received in accordance with the progress it has achieved in this regard.
3. To undertake to finance social security networks and provide the necessary finance for small and medium-sized projects.
4. To instruct the Ministerial Councils and specialist Arab organisations in co-ordination with the Secretariat General to follow up the implementation of the programme and present a report to the Summit on the progress achieved.

Q.Q:11D.A(1)-J4, dated 20/1/2009

The Development of Education in the Arab Nation

The Council of the League at Summit level has studied the following:

• The memorandum of the Secretariat General
• The report of the Secretary General to the Arab Economic, Development and Social Summit
• The resolutions of the Arab Summit related to the development of education in the Arab nation
• The report and resolutions of the Economic and Social Council at its Extraordinary Session held on 2–4 December 2008

– The Council confirms the resolutions of the Arab Summits held in Khartoum in 2006, Riyadh in 2007 and Damascus in 2008 regarding the development of education in the Arab nation.

– It affirms the importance of education in the Arab nation as a principal component for comprehensive development in Arab countries and raising the standard of living of Arab citizens.

– It indicates the necessity of attending to the implementation of the objectives, means and programmes recorded in the education development plan in the Arab nation.

The Council resolves:

1. That Arab countries should implement the plan for the development of education in the Arab nation within the period 2009–19, and that every country should act to increase the budget of its Ministry of Education and allocate all the necessary resources for the plan.
2. To support the efforts of the Secretariat General and the Arab League Educational, Cultural and Scientific Organisation for the execution of the plan, its programmes and projects, and it instructs them to prepare periodic reports on the progress achieved in this respect and refer them to the Summit.

Q.Q:12D.A(1)-J4, dated 20/1/2009

Improvement of the Level of Health Care

The Council of the League at Summit level has studied the following:

• The memorandum of the Secretariat General
• The report of the Secretary General to the Arab Economic, Development and Social Summit
• The resolutions issued by the Arab Summit related to the development and improvement of health care
• The report and resolutions of the Economic and Social Council at its Extraordinary Session held on 2–4 December 2008

– The Council insists on improvements of the level of public health for citizens of Arab countries, the unification of Arab efforts in various health fields, and adherence to international strategies for food supply and healthy physical activity.

– It is aware of the importance of developing health institutions in the member countries and action to improve performance in accordance with recognised quality standards.

– It applauds the achievements of the member countries in eliminating the spread of infectious diseases and is aware of the importance of combating non-infectious diseases, in particular diabetes, whose rate of incidence in Arab countries has increased rapidly.

The Council resolves:

1. That the governments of Arab countries should continue to improve the level of primary health care services and implement the pattern of family medicine in their countries, and should put this at the top of the priorities of the programme of Arab Ministries of Health, and it instructs the Council of Arab Ministers of Health to prepare a comprehensive Arab programme in this regard.
2. To allocate the necessary financial resources to the Ministries of Health in each country in accordance with the international standards of the World Health Organisation in this regard.
3. To instruct the Council of Arab Ministers of Health to present the Summit with periodic reports on the progress achieved in this regard.

Q.Q:13D.A(1)-J4, dated 20/1/2009

The Role of the Private Sector in Supporting Joint Arab Action

The Council of the League at Summit level has studied the following:

• The memorandum of the Secretariat General
• The report of the Secretary General to the Arab Economic, Development and Social Summit
• The paper of the General Federation of Chambers of Commerce, Agriculture and Industry of Arab countries regarding the vision and requirements of the private sector to achieve Arab economic integration

– The Council values the efforts and effective participation of the private sector in preparing for the Economic, Development and Social Summit.

The Council resolves:

1. To give its blessing to the efforts of the Arab private sector in support of joint Arab action, and it invites it to continue to support the path of Arab economic development.
2. To support the participation of the private sector in the implementation of national economic development projects and joint Arab projects to strengthen joint Arab economic activity.
3. To strengthen the participation of the private sector in following up the

implementation of the resolutions issued by the Economic, Developmental and Social Summit in co-operation with the League of Arab States.

Q.Q:14D.A(1)-J4, dated 20/1/2009

Encouragement of the Role of Arab Organisations in Civil Society

The Council of the League at Summit level has studied the following:

• The memorandum of the Secretariat General
• The report of the Secretary General to the Arab Economic, Development and Social Summit

– The Council affirms the role of social participation in the achievement of the economic and social development programmes.

– It notes the increasing role of Arab organisations in civil society in numerous areas of public life.

– It takes cognizance of the resolution of the Council of the League at Summit level, no. 280 D.A. (16), dated 23/5/2004, regarding the development of the Economic and Social Council, and Resolution 433 D.A. (20), dated 30/3/2008, regarding support for the encouragement of the role of Arab institutions in civil society.

The Council resolves:

1. To encourage the role of civil society in various economic, social and development fields and the strengthening of collaboration with its organisations and institutions to achieve the developmental, economic and social objectives in the member countries.
2. To support the efforts of Arab organisations in the civil society at regional and international levels, and in particular their activities that seek to promote the Arab identity.

Q.Q:15D.A(1)-J4, dated 20/1/2009

Appendix 2

The resolutions of the G20 Summit, London, 2 April 2009

Global Plan for Recovery and Reform
Statement issued by the G20 Leaders, London, 2 April 2009
Source: www.imf.org/external/np/sec/pr/2009/pdf/g20_040209.pdf

1. We, the Leaders of the Group of Twenty, met in London on 2 April 2009.

2. We face the greatest challenge to the world economy in modern times; a crisis which has deepened since we last met, which affects the lives of men, women and children in every country, and which all countries must join together to resolve. A global crisis requires a global solution.

3. We start from the belief that prosperity is indivisible; that growth, to be sustained, has to be shared; and that our global plan for recovery must have at its heart the needs and jobs of hard-working families, not just in developed countries but in emerging markets and the poorest countries of the world too; and must reflect the interests, not just of today's population, but of future generations too. We believe that the only sure foundation for sustainable globalisation and rising prosperity for all is an open world economy based on market principles, effective regulation, and strong global institutions.

4. We have today therefore pledged to do whatever is necessary to:
   - restore confidence, growth, and jobs;
   - repair the financial system to restore lending;
   - strengthen financial regulation to rebuild trust;
   - fund and reform our international financial institutions to overcome this crisis and prevent future ones;
   - promote global trade and investment and reject protectionism, to underpin prosperity; and
   - build an inclusive, green, and sustainable recovery.

   By acting together to fulfil these pledges we will bring the world economy out of recession and prevent a crisis like this from recurring in the future.

5. The agreements we have reached today, to treble resources available to the IMF to $750 billion, to support a new SDR allocation of $250 billion, to support at least $100 billion of additional lending by the MDBs, to ensure $250 billion of support for trade finance, and to use the additional resources from agreed IMF gold sales for concessional finance for the poorest countries, constitute an additional $1.1 trillion programme of support to restore credit, growth and jobs in the world economy. Together with the measures we have each taken nationally, this constitutes a global plan for recovery on an unprecedented scale.

Restoring growth and jobs

6. We are undertaking an unprecedented and concerted fiscal expansion, which will save or create millions of jobs which would otherwise have been destroyed, and that will, by the end of next year, amount to $5 trillion, raise output by 4 percent, and accelerate the transition to a green economy. We are committed to deliver the scale of sustained fiscal effort necessary to restore growth.

7. Our central banks have also taken exceptional action. Interest rates have been cut aggressively in most countries, and our central banks have pledged to maintain expansionary policies for as long as needed and to use the full range of monetary policy instruments, including unconventional instruments, consistent with price stability.

8. Our actions to restore growth cannot be effective until we restore domestic lending and international capital flows. We have provided significant and

comprehensive support to our banking systems to provide liquidity, recapitalise financial institutions, and address decisively the problem of impaired assets. We are committed to take all necessary actions to restore the normal flow of credit through the financial system and ensure the soundness of systemically important institutions, implementing our policies in line with the agreed G20 framework for restoring lending and repairing the financial sector.

9. Taken together, these actions will constitute the largest fiscal and monetary stimulus and the most comprehensive support programme for the financial sector in modern times. Acting together strengthens the impact and the exceptional policy actions announced so far must be implemented without delay. Today, we have further agreed over $1 trillion of additional resources for the world economy through our international financial institutions and trade finance.

10. Last month the IMF estimated that world growth in real terms would resume and rise to over 2 percent by the end of 2010. We are confident that the actions we have agreed today, and our unshakeable commitment to work together to restore growth and jobs, while preserving long-term fiscal sustainability, will accelerate the return to trend growth. We commit today to taking whatever action is necessary to secure that outcome, and we call on the IMF to assess regularly the actions taken and the global actions required.

11. We are resolved to ensure long-term fiscal sustainability and price stability and will put in place credible exit strategies from the measures that need to be taken now to support the financial sector and restore global demand. We are convinced that by implementing our agreed policies we will limit the longer-term costs to our economies, thereby reducing the scale of the fiscal consolidation necessary over the longer term.

12. We will conduct all our economic policies co-operatively and responsibly with regard to the impact on other countries and will refrain from competitive devaluation of our currencies and promote a stable and well-functioning international monetary system. We will submit, now and in the future, to candid, even-handed, and independent IMF surveillance of our economies and financial sectors, of the impact of our policies on others, and of risks facing the global economy.

Strengthening financial supervision and regulation

13. Major failures in the financial sector and in financial regulation and supervision were fundamental causes of the crisis. Confidence will not be restored until we rebuild trust in our financial system. We will take action to build a stronger, more globally consistent, supervisory and regulatory framework for the future financial sector, which will support sustainable global growth and serve the needs of business and citizens.

14. We each agree to ensure our domestic regulatory systems are strong. But we also agree to establish the much greater consistency and systematic co-operation between countries, and the framework of internationally agreed high standards, that a global financial system requires. Strengthened regulation and supervision must promote propriety, integrity and transparency; guard against risk across the financial system; dampen rather than amplify the financial and economic cycle; reduce reliance on inappropriately risky sources of financing; and discourage excessive risk-taking. Regulators and supervisors must protect consumers and investors, support market discipline, avoid adverse impacts on other countries, reduce the scope for regulatory arbitrage, support competition and dynamism, and keep pace with innovation in the marketplace.

15. To this end we are implementing the Action Plan agreed at our last meeting, as set out in the attached progress report. We have today also issued a Declaration, *Strengthening the Financial System*. In particular we agree:

    • to establish a new Financial Stability Board (FSB) with a strengthened mandate, as a successor to the Financial Stability Forum (FSF), including all G20 countries, FSF members, Spain, and the European Commission;
    • that the FSB should collaborate with the IMF to provide early warning of macroeconomic and financial risks and the actions needed to address them; to reshape our regulatory systems so that our authorities are able to identify and take account of macro-prudential risks;
    • to extend regulation and oversight to all systemically important financial institutions, instruments and markets. This will include, for the first time, systemically important hedge funds;
    • to endorse and implement the FSF's tough new principles on pay and compensation and to support sustainable compensation schemes and the corporate social responsibility of all firms;
    • to take action, once recovery is assured, to improve the quality, quantity,

and international consistency of capital in the banking system. In future, regulation must prevent excessive leverage and require buffers of resources to be built up in good times;

- to take action against non-co-operative jurisdictions, including tax havens. We stand ready to deploy sanctions to protect our public finances and financial systems. The era of banking secrecy is over. We note that the OECD has today published a list of countries assessed by the Global Forum against the international standard for exchange of tax information;

- to call on the accounting standard setters to work urgently with supervisors and regulators to improve standards on valuation and provisioning and achieve a single set of high-quality global accounting standards; and

- to extend regulatory oversight and registration to Credit Rating Agencies to ensure they meet the international code of good practice, particularly to prevent unacceptable conflicts of interest.

16. We instruct our Finance Ministers to complete the implementation of these decisions in line with the timetable set out in the Action Plan. We have asked the FSB and the IMF to monitor progress, working with the Financial Action Taskforce and other relevant bodies, and to provide a report to the next meeting of our Finance Ministers in Scotland in November.

Strengthening our global financial institutions

17. Emerging markets and developing countries, which have been the engine of recent world growth, are also now facing challenges which are adding to the current downturn in the global economy. It is imperative for global confidence and economic recovery that capital continues to flow to them. This will require a substantial strengthening of the international financial institutions, particularly the IMF. We have therefore agreed today to make available an additional $850 billion of resources through the global financial institutions to support growth in emerging markets and developing countries by helping to finance counter-cyclical spending, bank recapitalisation, infrastructure, trade finance, balance of payments support, debt rollover, and social support. To this end:

- we have agreed to increase the resources available to the IMF through immediate financing from members of $250 billion, subsequently incorporated into an expanded and more flexible New Arrangements to Borrow, increased by up to $500 billion, and to consider market borrowing if necessary; and

- we support a substantial increase in lending of at least $100 billion by the Multilateral Development Banks (MDBs), including to low income countries, and ensure that all MDBs, including have the appropriate capital [*sic*].

18. It is essential that these resources can be used effectively and flexibly to support growth. We welcome in this respect the progress made by the IMF with its new Flexible Credit Line (FCL) and its reformed lending and conditionality framework which will enable the IMF to ensure that its facilities address effectively the underlying causes of countries' balance of payments financing needs, particularly the withdrawal of external capital flows to the banking and corporate sectors. We support Mexico's decision to seek an FCL arrangement.

19. We have agreed to support a general SDR allocation which will inject $250 billion into the world economy and increase global liquidity, and urgent ratification of the Fourth Amendment.

20. In order for our financial institutions to help manage the crisis and prevent future crises we must strengthen their longer-term relevance, effectiveness and legitimacy. So alongside the significant increase in resources agreed today we are determined to reform and modernise the international financial institutions to ensure they can assist members and shareholders effectively in the new challenges they face. We will reform their mandates, scope and governance to reflect changes in the world economy and the new challenges of globalisation, and that emerging and developing economies, including the poorest, must have greater voice and representation. This must be accompanied by action to increase the credibility and accountability of the institutions through better strategic oversight and decision making. To this end:

- we commit to implementing the package of IMF quota and voice reforms agreed in April 2008 and call on the IMF to complete the next review of quotas by January 2011;
- we agree that, alongside this, consideration should be given to greater involvement of the Fund's Governors in providing strategic direction to the IMF and increasing its accountability;

- we commit to implementing the World Bank reforms agreed in October 2008. We look forward to further recommendations, at the next meetings, on voice and representation reforms on an accelerated timescale, to be agreed by the 2010 Spring Meetings;
- we agree that the heads and senior leadership of the international financial institutions should be appointed through an open, transparent, and merit-based selection process; and
- building on the current reviews of the IMF and World Bank we asked the Chairman, working with the G20 Finance Ministers, to consult widely in an inclusive process and report back to the next meeting with proposals for further reforms to improve the responsiveness and adaptability of the IFIs.

21. In addition to reforming our international financial institutions for the new challenges of globalisation we agreed on the desirability of a new global consensus on the key values and principles that will promote sustainable economic activity. We support discussion on such a charter for sustainable economic activity with a view to further discussion at our next meeting. We take note of the work started in other fora in this regard and look forward to further discussion of this charter for sustainable economic activity.

Resisting protectionism and promoting global trade and investment

22. World trade growth has underpinned rising prosperity for half a century. But it is now falling for the first time in 25 years. Falling demand is exacerbated by growing protectionist pressures and a withdrawal of trade credit. Reinvigorating world trade and investment is essential for restoring global growth. We will not repeat the historic mistakes of protectionism of previous eras. To this end:

- we reaffirm the commitment made in Washington: to refrain from raising new barriers to investment or to trade in goods and services, imposing new export restrictions, or implementing World Trade Organisation (WTO) inconsistent measures to stimulate exports. In addition we will rectify promptly any such measures. We extend this pledge to the end of 2010;
- we will minimise any negative impact on trade and investment of our

domestic policy actions including fiscal policy and action in support of the financial sector. We will not retreat into financial protectionism, particularly measures that constrain worldwide capital flows, especially to developing countries;

- we will notify promptly the WTO of any such measures and we call on the WTO, together with other international bodies, within their respective mandates, to monitor and report publicly on our adherence to these undertakings on a quarterly basis;
- we will take, at the same time, whatever steps we can to promote and facilitate trade and investment; and
- we will ensure availability of at least $250 billion over the next two years to support trade finance through our export credit and investment agencies and through the MDBs. We also ask our regulators to make use of available flexibility in capital requirements for trade finance.

23. We remain committed to reaching an ambitious and balanced conclusion to the Doha Development Round, which is urgently needed. This could boost the global economy by at least $150 billion per annum. To achieve this we are committed to building on the progress already made, including with regard to modalities.

24. We will give renewed focus and political attention to this critical issue in the coming period and will use our continuing work and all international meetings that are relevant to drive progress.

Ensuring a fair and sustainable recovery for all

25. We are determined not only to restore growth but to lay the foundation for a fair and sustainable world economy. We recognise that the current crisis has a disproportionate impact on the vulnerable in the poorest countries and recognise our collective responsibility to mitigate the social impact of the crisis to minimise long-lasting damage to global potential. To this end:

- we reaffirm our historic commitment to meeting the Millennium Development Goals and to achieving our respective ODA pledges, including commitments on Aid for Trade, debt relief, and the Gleneagles commitments, especially to sub-Saharan Africa;
- the actions and decisions we have taken today will provide $50 billion to support social protection, boost trade and safeguard development in low

income countries, as part of the significant increase in crisis support for these and other developing countries and emerging markets;

- we are making available resources for social protection for the poorest countries, including through investing in long-term food security and through voluntary bilateral contributions to the World Bank's Vulnerability Framework, including the Infrastructure Crisis Facility, and the Rapid Social Response Fund;
- we have committed, consistent with the new income model, that additional resources from agreed sales of IMF gold will be used, together with surplus income, to provide $6 billion additional concessional and flexible finance for the poorest countries over the next 2 to 3 years. We call on the IMF to come forward with concrete proposals at the Spring Meetings;
- we have agreed to review the flexibility of the Debt Sustainability Framework and call on the IMF and World Bank to report to the IMFC and Development Committee at the Annual Meetings; and
- we call on the UN, working with other global institutions, to establish an effective mechanism to monitor the impact of the crisis on the poorest and most vulnerable.

26. We recognise the human dimension to the crisis. We commit to support those affected by the crisis by creating employment opportunities and through income support measures. We will build a fair and family-friendly labour market for both women and men. We therefore welcome the reports of the London Jobs Conference and the Rome Social Summit and the key principles they proposed. We will support employment by stimulating growth, investing in education and training, and through active labour market policies, focusing on the most vulnerable. We call upon the ILO, working with other relevant organisations, to assess the actions taken and those required for the future.

27. We agreed to make the best possible use of investment funded by fiscal stimulus programmes towards the goal of building a resilient, sustainable, and green recovery. We will make the transition towards clean, innovative, resource efficient, low carbon technologies and infrastructure. We encourage the MDBs to contribute fully to the achievement of this objective. We will identify and work together on further measures to build sustainable economies.

28. We reaffirm our commitment to address the threat of irreversible climate change, based on the principle of common but differentiated responsibilities, and to reach agreement at the UN Climate Change conference in Copenhagen in December 2009.

Delivering our commitments

29. We have committed ourselves to work together with urgency and determination to translate these words into action. We agreed to meet again before the end of this year to review progress on our commitments.

Appendix 3

The internet and mortgage crises

2000
- A sharp fall on Wall Street in the value of shares in the new economy, in particular dotcom and information technology companies

2001
- Debt crisis explodes in Argentina following the refusal of the International Monetary Fund to grant $1.2 billion of urgent assistance
- US giant Enron collapses

2002
- WorldCom telecommunications corporation goes bankrupt

2007
- First hint of the sub-prime mortgage crisis with the announcement by HSBC that the unrecovered loans in risky real estate amounting to $10.5 billion would be provided for out of profits alone
- New Century real estate company declares bankruptcy
- Collapse of the US real estate loans market exposed to sub-prime risk – the start of the financial crisis

2007–08
- Governments in a number of countries begin to pump funds into and

provide guarantees for banks and devise plans to revive the economy with hundreds of billions

2008
- Global stock markets begin to tumble
- The US Congress votes on the plan to rescue the US real estate market with a sum of $300 million
- The US government nationalises Fannie Mae and Freddie Mac, two giant secondary mortgage corporations on the brink of bankruptcy
- Lehman Brothers goes bankrupt
- Bank of America buys Merrill Lynch
- The US Federal Reserve and the US government buy approximately 80 percent of the capital in the insurance company American International Group (AIG) for $85 billion
- Investment banks Goldman Sachs and Morgan Stanley converted into commercial banks to benefit from the American rescue plan
- US Congress adopts the amended rescue plan costing $700 billion
- Britain, Germany, France and Italy undertake to co-ordinate and take joint action to rescue the financial system
- An international Summit takes place to discuss the crisis, bringing together the G20 and attended by the Kingdom of Saudi Arabia as representative of the Arabs

2009
- The Obama plan to revive the US economy at a cost of $825 billion

Appendix 4

Extracts from the Professional Code
of Ethics for Quebec Journalists

**The Professional Federation of Journalists in Quebec/
Fédération professionnelle des journalistes du Québec (FPJQ)**

This code of professional conduct was adopted by the general meeting of the Federation of Professional Journalists in Quebec on 24 November 1996.

Below are extracts of its most important provisions. The full text is available at http://www.fpjq.org/index.php?id=97

Preamble

The role of journalists is to accurately report, analyse, and in some cases, comment on the facts that help their fellow citizens understand the world in which they live.

Complete, exact and diverse information is one of the most important guarantees of freedom and democracy.

When information is of public interest, it must always circulate freely. Facts and ideas must be communicated without constraint or obstacle. Knowing that a free press acts as an indispensable watchdog over authority and institutions, journalists must defend the freedom of the press and the public's right to information; they must fight any restrictions, pressures and threats that aim to limit the gathering and dissemination of information.

Journalists serve the public interest – not personal or specific interests. As such, they have a responsibility to publish everything that is of public interest. This obligation must override any desire to serve information sources or to favour the financial and competitive needs of news organisations.

Journalists must take their role very seriously. They must demand of themselves the same ethical qualities they demand of newsmakers; in other words, they cannot denounce other people's conflicts of interest, and at the same time, accept their own.

This Code establishes the ethical rules that should guide journalistic work. These rules lay the foundation for a journalist's most precious asset: credibility.

Since it takes into account the specific nature of the journalistic environment, this is not a Code in the strictest sense of the word.

1. Definition

The term "journalist" in this Code refers to all people who exercise a journalistic function for a news organisation. In the context of publicly disseminating information or opinions, this includes one or several of the following tasks: researching, reporting, interviewing; writing or preparing reports, analyses, commentaries, or specialised columns; translating or adapting texts; press photography, filmed or electronic reports; assignment, the desk (headlines, lay-out ...), editing; caricatures; information drawing and graphics; animation, producing and supervising current affairs programs and films; managing news, public affairs or other comparable departments.

2. Fundamental journalistic values

The fundamental values of journalists include: a critical viewpoint, so they methodically doubt everything; impartiality, so they research and expose the diverse aspects of a given situation; fairness, so they view all citizens as equal before the press as they are before the law; independence, so they maintain their distance from authority and lobby groups; public respect and compassion, so they demonstrate moderation; honesty, so they display a scrupulous respect for facts and are open-minded. This in turn demonstrates a receptiveness to unfamiliar realities, and an ability to report on these realities without prejudice.

3. Truth and rigour

3a Accuracy

Journalists must rigorously gather and verify information to ensure their facts are accurate. They must correct their mistakes diligently and appropriately with regard to the harm they have caused.

3b Context

Journalists must put their facts and opinions in their proper context so they are understandable, without exaggerating or diminishing their scope.

3c Headlines

Headlines and introductions of articles and news reports should not exaggerate or lead to misinterpretation.

3d Personal opinions

So as not to confuse the public, journalists must carefully distinguish between personal opinions, analysis and factual information. Above all, they must give a precise account of the facts. In the case of editorials, columns and opinion pieces, or in advocacy journalism where opinions dominate, journalists must also respect the facts.

3e Rumours

A rumour cannot be published unless it originates from a credible source and contributes to the understanding of an event. It must always be identified as a rumour. In the judicial field, the publication of rumours is prohibited.

3f Quotations

Journalists must give an accurate account of what people say. Quotations, editing, sound effects, etc, and the sequence in which they are presented, must not distort the meaning of people's words.

3g Images

Photographs, graphics, sounds and images that are published or broadcast must represent reality as accurately as possible. Artistic concerns should not result in public deception. Edited images and photographs must be identified as such.

3h Plagiarism

Journalists must never plagiarise. If they use an exclusive piece of information that has just been published or broadcast by another media organisation, they must identify the source.

9. Conflicts of interest

9c Gifts and other rewards

Journalists must refuse gifts and other rewards that may be offered as a result of their duties. Gifts should be returned to the senders with an explanation

Accepting gifts compromises journalistic impartiality or the appearance of impartiality. Gifts do not constitute a normal benefit of the journalistic profession.

Gifts are only acceptable when they serve a direct purpose in journalistic work: books; records; free tickets to cover exhibits and shows; in the case of consumer journalism, certain objects, etc. After being used, and unless they are being kept for reference purposes, these objects should be given to community or public organisations whenever possible.

A gift can also be acceptable when its value is of little importance, and when the cost of returning it to the sender exceeds the cost of the object.

9e Paid trips

Journalists and media must pay the costs associated with covering their stories. They must not accept free trips or financial aid from public or private organisations that are seeking media coverage

Trips that are paid by sources can distort coverage by favouring wealthy interest groups. They can also – at least in appearance – limit journalists' freedom of expression. A trip offered by a source can nonetheless be accepted:

• when there is no other way of obtaining information or no other way of travelling to the site. In this case, the media organisation should evaluate and reimburse the cost of the trip;

• when the trip provides professional training and is not used to gather stories.

If – in exceptional circumstances and as a last resort – media organisations accept a trip paid by a source, journalists must protect their professional freedom while covering the story. In addition, they must explicitly inform the public that their trips were paid by a source.

Appendix 5

Mohamed Bin Issa Al Jaber

Extracts from the interview published in *Al-Iqtisad wa-'l-A'maal*
(Economics and Business Magazine), no. 349, January 2009,
Beirut, Lebanon

• What qualities would you say have been the ones propelling Mohamed Bin
Issa Al Jaber, a self-made businessman, to the top of a large and multi-faceted
international business group within thirty years?

– My constant guide has been my firm resolve to rely on three vital principles:
self-reliance, holding fast to specific aims and ambitions, and the wisdom to
benefit from the experiences and successes of others. This has been the *raison
d'être* of our presence in Europe over the last twenty-five years. I believed that
I had to achieve my objectives by being open in all my dealings and by getting
my message across clearly. We were transparent, a crucial factor in dealing with
others. In my opinion it is important not to take rash decisions and to be
strictly truthful in one's relationships. These are the foremost human qualities.
It is also important to stay level-headed and eschew extremes of behaviour.
Our societies suffer from exaggerated egotism and emotion, and many of us
would agree with the pre-Islamic poet 'Amr ibn Kalthoum when he said:

Let no one compete with us in folly. We are more foolish than the folly of fools.

141

Praise be to God. Since our business began thirty years ago we have no reason to regret or feel angry about anything, past or future. We have always held aloof from risk or anything that might limit our options. That is the source of the strength characteristic of our group and typical of its personality. We have nothing to fear. Transparency has been our watchword and we have worked with expert international firms in managing our business. We still deal with the same international businesses twenty-five years on, and these firms, whether financial or commercial, that have helped us, have confidence in us.

Our partners have stuck with us throughout all our operations, so that our relationship has gained strength through mutual trust. That is our distinguishing feature. I am totally confident that no group or businessman relying on these principles will fail, and have no doubt about this as the recipe for success. In brief: self-confidence, reliance on expertise, transparency, resolve, adherence to the law, and abiding by the law oneself first of all so that one can apply it to others.

• How would you describe your personality? What do you regard as your strengths and weaknesses?

– My basic weakness has always been my high level of good faith and excessive trust in people. I suffer from this even now. My strengths are clarity of vision, truthfulness in my dealings, and scepticism of unrealistic aspirations and fantasies. This sets me apart from most people, who tend to be over-optimistic and inclined to take more risks.

Risk-taking is certainly a part of running any business. However it must be calculated risk-taking. If it is not, it is in my view a fatal flaw. This can cause problems with other people, who often think I am criticising them when really I am only giving them advice. Good advice is seemingly not always welcome, and people do not learn from others' experiences. "Advice is unwelcome even if it drops from the lips like pearls." We have certainly learned much from our own experiences, but we have learned even more from the experiences of others.

• How would you summarise your business philosophy and your relationships with people, and especially relationships involving business interests?

– Showing the highest respect possible for others' interests is a sign that you have equal respect for your own. You will never succeed if you are foolhardy or if you ignore the interests of others. Any business and any agreement between two parties must be based on this principle, as well as on good faith and transparency.

• Nevertheless, don't your personality and your business methods sometimes cause controversy?

– That may be so. The reason is because I express my criticisms, and don't hide my feelings or indulge in flattery. This is where I differ from others. Some of my criticisms in the past have been regarded as harsh because they have been directed at projects, plans and ambitions on which great hopes have been riding, whereas I make realistic and genuine advice my starting point, so this may be the cause. People only like to hear what they want to hear.

• What is your assessment of your experience in the Kingdom of Saudi Arabia? And how much business are you doing there these days?

– It has been and continues to be a good and enriching experience given where I started from. It currently represents about 23 percent of Group turnover.

• How extensive are your Arab investments, and in general how is the investment portfolio of the Group distributed geographically?

– Sadly Arab investments by our Group are very few. Outside Saudi Arabia we have a presence only in Egypt, where our investments to the end of the current year constitute about 7 percent of total Group investment, and they have declined slightly. We currently have plans to expand into foodstuffs and the food and agriculture industries.

• Are you contemplating new investments and projects in the Arab region?

– Our ongoing operations in Europe are perhaps the main reason for our lack of expansion in the Arab world. Until 2011 we shall be confining our interests to foodstuffs.

• What is the current structure of the Mohamed Bin Issa Al Jaber Group (MBI)? How are its activities spread among the various sectors and markets?

– MBI Group activities are distributed over four main sectors. These are the hotel and tourism sector, which with its recent expansion has become the largest in Europe, followed by property investments, then foodstuffs and agricultural industries, and then petroleum investments. Foodstuffs are among our plans for expansion in the Arab world along with the oil and gas sector.

• What is the reason for this negative attitude towards investment in the region?

– It may perhaps be because our business over the last seven years has grown mostly in Europe while it has not developed to the same extent in the Arab world. 30 percent of our investments are in the Arab world and perhaps it is our major involvement in Europe that has distracted us from concentrating more on investing in Arab countries. Nothing can alter the fact that they are close to my heart and that I am myself of Arab origin. However business and finance should not be swayed by emotion.

• You have invested in Saudi Arabia and Egypt. What are the most important lessons you have drawn from your experience of investing in the region?

– My experience differs from one country to another. The economy in Saudi Arabia has always been a free-market, non-dirigiste one. Hence there are more attractive opportunities there and it is easier to achieve one's aims. Egypt of course passed through many phases until the beginning of the 1990s when it began to adopt free-market policies, and it has gone on to develop more recently at the end of the 1990s and by leaps and bounds at the beginning of this century. It has made great progress in the last five years, perhaps equal to its progress in its whole previous history. This has naturally made a big difference. The Kingdom of Saudi Arabia too has taken great strides in recent years in encouraging investment, investment that has been encouraged by its originally open economic environment. I believe that it has made great advances. Naturally there are differences between these two markets, but there is no doubt they are new and promising ones. However, much depends on the quality of what one is buying into. Investing in the region demands hands-on management and continuous personal effort, whereas the situation is completely different in other countries, because they are based on institutions.

• In the light of this experience what advice would you give to investors in the region?

– My advice would be directed at the people of the region but not at outsiders. I would advise them not to be influenced by hyperbole and not to rush headlong into projects and dreams that may not be realistic or practical, or too big to be absorbed by the economy. Today there are grave dangers facing Arab citizens hoping for a rise in their income and standard of living.

My first concern is for these citizens' circumstances. I have spoken out on previous occasions about various organisations, and have perhaps been hard on them, but the reality now proves that I was not overstating the case or too severe in my assessment. But I was fearful and angry all at once.

• You are not in favour of investment in the region, an attitude that surprises many, and there are those who consider it inappropriate and unfair, especially in view of the massive transformations and reforms in most countries in the region that have created a beneficial investment environment, and also in view of many successful investments in numerous Arab markets.

– I wish this interview were not taking place at this unfortunate time for markets in the Arab region and around the world. However the Arab region concerns me because the US and European economies will bounce back faster than the Arab ones. I am sorry not to give a complete answer to the question, because I do not wish to be harsh while all this is going on, and shall pass rapidly over a number of important points. Events in the region over the last five years, a time that has seen a surge in high incomes, have led to very high rates of inflation and a sharp rise in the cost of living, and dreams have begun to collapse. This is extremely sad.

Governments generally are entrusted with the leading role in the management of the economy. They should therefore have intervened to prevent matters reaching their current sorry state. In saying this I'm not criticising governments, but I am saying that some businessmen have promoted pipedreams out of all proportion to reality. Their motive, most unfortunately, has been celebrity and a desire to appear all-knowing.

In most cases the problem has been a lack of prior experience, which has led the region's markets into their difficult predicament. We should not lay the blame for all our problems on others. We should be rational and hold ourselves accountable, and take responsibility for our mistakes and lay the blame on those who have really caused the problems. Perhaps we have already begun to feel the effects of these mistakes but their real consequences will unfold over the next two years.

There may well be a lot of arrogant optimists who are in a state of denial, but a start must be made now to seek a way out and examine in depth ways to rebuild the structure from within, and to protect small investors and small dealers in shares, property and so on. The elite who bear responsibility fall into a different category, because they are partly to blame for all this irresponsibility. They have been reckless and refuse to admit it.

• What do you say about the massive losses sustained by Arab and other investors in foreign markets in all types of shares: property, bonds, banks and others?

– Everything can be controlled except for greed. The greedier people are the more they lose. I have not been involved in Arab and foreign stock markets over the last five years. Furthermore most of the losses were in indirect investments based on promises and bits of paper that were presented as secure and guaranteed. I am not trying to parade my experience, but I will say that I am as I am today because I saw the crisis coming five years ago. I turned away completely from stock markets and have had no involvement in them since 2003. All my investments are direct ones, and I tend to avoid indirect investing because I do not participate in projects I'm uncertain about. Furthermore I am not easily persuaded that others can create wealth for me, because in most cases it involves relying on someone else, who may be guided by different calculations.

Naturally I have benefited greatly from others in what I have done and learned over the last three decades. At the end of the 1970s, and at the beginning of the 1980s and 1990s, I was very aware of frequent fluctuations. At that time I was in the stock market. I had not read much about it and although the fluctuations were not as extreme as those causing so much pain today, it was reminiscent of the economic crisis of the 1930s. Now I am a direct investor and do not believe in indirect investment. I avoid relying on others and have turned my back on the stock market five years ago. I apply to myself what I criticise others for. I expected my criticisms and arguments with other people to result in some correction to price fluctuations, but instead they got bigger.

• Why have you turned towards Europe, and how did your experience in Western markets develop?

– Markets in the West have developed over the past 250 years and have built up a rich store of experience. In truth I benefited and continue to benefit from this just as I benefit from all successful experiences. Winning formulae provide

146

recipes for success. To begin from absolutely nothing and to rely upon intuition in disregard of the lessons of experience can only lead to extreme misfortune.

• What are the factors that led you to turn to the hotels sector and expand within it?

– We, as a Group, began in property development twenty-eight years ago. After 1986 we began to invest in the hotels sector in Portugal. The idea came to me a long time ago. In 1989 we decided to form the JJW Company specifically for hotels and we started off in France. We began with four hotels that were built and developed by the Group, and today we have more than sixty hotels in the Group portfolio, 95 percent of them in Europe, in particular France, Britain, Austria and Portugal. Until the end of 2007 these countries accounted for approximately equal shares in our portfolio, each having between 24 and 26 percent. However after the recent deal, France has come to represent 60 percent of the hotels in the Group.

• Which part of the hotel market has the Group specialised in? Is it 4-star, 3-star, or average-cost hotels? Hotels for businessmen, or hotels for tourists? What are the distinguishing features of the Group's hotel product?

– France is the only country where the Group had and still has 3- and 4-star hotels. However at the end of 2008 the Group decided to dispose of the 3-star hotels and to retain the luxury ones, that is the 4-star or 4-star luxury hotels according to the French rating system, that is the equivalent of 5-star hotels in other countries. As for 6- and 7-star hotels, France does not believe in them, and neither do I.

• What is the composition of the Group's hotel network?

– We have a separate administration in each country, so that for example in France the company is French and operates according to French law. The same is true in Britain, Austria and Portugal. However the Group has a financial and administrative supervision office in Britain. So it can be called a multi-national group. There is no single nationality. Rather it includes companies of different nationalities: French, British, Austrian, Portuguese, Saudi Arabian and Egyptian.

• How does the Group rate its experience of direct management of the hotels?

Has it in fact succeeded in creating a commercial hotel brand like the well-known hotel groups?

– We have retained the personality, name, brand and history of each hotel. Among them are historic hotels a century or more old. This is certainly a reason for the hotels' success and their guests' loyalty to the hotel they are used to. Direct management means direct daily management, and there is an office in each capital to manage all the hotels in that country. The total number of workers in the hotels in the Group, following completion of the recent deal, will be 4,000 employees in the coming year.

• What is the level of the Group's indebtedness to the banks?

– The Group's debts do not exceed 25 percent of its book assets. As for its market assets, these were valued after all the falls in value in the property market, and there is an actual evaluation that indicates that the level of our indebtedness is much less in relation to market value.

• What is the level of income achieved by the Group from its business last year?

– Group profits during 2007 exceeded $400 million.

• What is the impact of the current crisis on the Group's ability to obtain cash and facilities from the international banking system?

– Our Group assets continue to be attractive to all the banks, even in these difficult times. This has enabled us to carry on in this market.

• What has been the impact of the liquidity crisis on the Group's finances and operations?

– I would like to stress again that the Group has been exposed to very little risk because of its extreme caution in low-risk investment. Neither the Group nor I personally have had any stock-market presence since 2003, nor have we engaged in speculation or volatile investments of any kind. We have stood aside from all of this. Thus our advice is formed by our own experience. That is why I think it best for those with an opinion to express not to be influenced by their own interests, so that their opinion can be impartial and objective. One should not seek advice about a particular financial market from someone in that market. Likewise in other areas of business, such as property development, an adviser should not be involved in trying to profit from it. I personally am extremely cautious about expressing my view on anything with which I am not directly familiar.

• What approach has your Group adopted to cope with the current economic and financial crisis?

– In this crisis we may perhaps find wisdom in the adage, 'One man's loss is another's gain'. Naturally we feel the pain of those who have suffered losses. However this crisis can also be an opportunity for others, including ourselves. We didn't wish for it, but it is perhaps an opportunity for us as a Group, as may be the case for many others. For example how did Rockefeller, Carnegie and others build their wealth? They bought in depressed markets, like those today, and in similar circumstances. So we look on this crisis as an opportunity.

• What are the Group's total assets, and are they valued by independent bodies?

– Yes, the Group's assets are subject to independent valuation. Up to the end of last October the value of the Group's assets was over $9 billion.

• How many people are directly employed by the Group?

– There are about 7,500.

• How does the profitability of the Group's subsidiary companies rate, and what are the best performing and most profitable companies in the Group?

– Last year the hotels were the most profitable. Of course the Continental Oil Company, which is an oil and gas business, is still at the stage of developing its assets, so its future profits may be different. Foodstuffs too are still growing and developing, but they may provide very large numbers in years to come.

I urge Arab businessmen to focus on food industries in the Arab world, because we are countries that import almost all our foodstuffs.

A few days ago we were discussing in the Group whether it was better to invest in the hotels sector or in property developments such as offices that we had decided to disengage from before. In my view a hotel may make a loss when there is a revenue crisis resulting from reservations being cancelled. By contrast, offices may have their entire leases cancelled. At any rate we have not been involved in this sector since 2006, but we do have a project in France that will not be ready before 2012.

• What is the composition of the company, the location of its registered office, and the legal and audit arrangements to which it is subject?

– It is a multinational company. It is British, French, Austrian, Portuguese, Saudi Arabian, Egyptian and American, with a head office in each country. However the central management office is in London.

• How can a concern the size of the Mohamed Bin Issa Al Jaber Group be effectively managed?

– As I indicated previously, the reason for our presence in Europe is to enable us to take advantage of readily available expertise. The Arab world today still lacks skills and competence. We have experts in the Group who have worked with us for more than twenty years. We have many staff who have worked in our head offices for more than ten or fifteen years. And of course we continually take on new expertise. There is no doubt that the Group has benefited from this diversification and from its presence in more than one country for over twenty years. As regards the management system, each in-country administration is fully and directly responsible for the management of the assets within that country. However they remain in constant communication with managements in the other countries, either through marketing, or information, or technology. They are all under the supervision and monitoring of the head office in London. There is centralisation and decentralisation all at once.

• What other management and human resources does the Group use in the management and planning of its business?

– I should certainly mention again our other partners with whom we have collaborated for many years, such as expert financial and legal firms, and major banks around the world. In the Group head office in London we have in-house financial controls trained at the top schools, but we also use external firms. Even though we do not deal with the stock exchange or international financial markets, our internal rules are similar to those of companies registered on them and we are more transparent than they are.

• Has the Group at any time considered floating its shares on the stock exchange? Can you give us some idea of the reasons that might lead to this step being taken? Where would the Group float its shares? Is this step still possible in the light of the adverse developments in the market?

– For seven years up to 2009 or 2010 we have been discussing taking such a step. We have now set the date. It will be at the end of 2011, when the shares will be floated on three stock exchanges – London, Paris and New York.

- No conversation with Sheikh Mohamed Bin Issa Al Jaber would be complete without exploring another important aspect of his life. This is his humanitarian work and concern for cultural and educational affairs. Out of regard for this UNESCO has appointed you as an envoy and the European Parliament has honoured you. The French government has also honoured you and a number of European universities have awarded you honorary doctorates. You have founded the MBI Al Jaber Foundation in London that engages in a wide range of cultural and educational activities, especially in providing scholarships for a large number of Arab students in European universities. Would you please say something about this Foundation?

– The existence of the Foundation derives from my absolute belief in social responsibility. This Foundation has served our sons and daughters in the Arab world, and despite my participation in cultural and educational work in both Europe and the Arab world, the Foundation's primary *raison d'être* is to serve the people of the Arab region. For more than ten years the Foundation has been awarding scholarships to Arab students to study in Britain, Austria or France. The aim is to select students who need scholarships. Our only stipulation is that they return to serve their home country. The Group has so far been honoured to serve hundreds of students from a range of Arab countries. Starting from last year the Foundation acquired a large share in MODUL University in Vienna and we allocated thirty-five annual scholarships to it. These are a gift to Arab countries for higher studies and specialisations in tourism and the hospitality business, to equip them to help develop this industry in the Arab world. This university teaches economics and other subjects as well as tourism.

The Foundation carries out other activities too in humanitarian, cultural and educational fields. We have established and continue to build all our relationships with others – with the West, for the benefit of our Arab society in Saudi Arabia, in the Gulf, in the Yemen and in all the Arab countries. All humanitarian manifestos proclaim the value of giving and urge people to give what they can to their society, their nation and to people in general. What we do is no more than a recognition of belonging.

I am happy and fulfilled by my participation in the Foundation's activities and in various other humanitarian and educational collaborations and projects aimed at educating our Arab compatriots, and at dialogue with and getting to know other people.

References

Principal references in Arabic

IBN HASSAN, Dr Musa bin Ja'far (1995), *Tatwir al-qanun al-idari al-'Umani* (The Development of the Omani Administrative Law). Oman: Al-Matabi' al-Dhahabiyya (The Golden Presses)

HIJAZI, Dr Mustafa (2006), *Al-insan al-mahdur* (Ruined Mankind). Casablanca: Al-Markaz al-Thaqafi al-'Arabi (The Arab Cultural Centre), 2nd impression

JA'AIT, Dr Hisham (1995), *Al-shakhsiyya al-'Arabiyya al-Islamiyya wa-'l-masir al-'Arabi* (The Arab-Islamic Personality and Arab Destiny). Translated into Arabic by Dr Al-Manji Al-Sayyadi. Beirut: Dar al-Tali'a, 2nd impression

JULIEN, Dr Charles-André (1969), *Ta'rikh Ifriqiyya al-Shamaliyya* (A History of North Africa). Translated into Arabic by Muhammad Mazali and Al-Bashir bin Salama. Tunis: Al-Dar al-Tunisiyya li'l-Nashr (Tunisian Publishing House)

MAHMOUD, Dr Zaki Naguib (1982), *Thaqafatuna fi muwajha al-'asr* (Our Culture Against This Age). Cairo: Dar al-Shurouq, 3rd impression

AL-YAZIJI, Dr Kamal (1979), *Ma'alim al-fikr al-'Arabi* (Signposts to Arab Thought). Beirut: Dar al-'Ilm li-'l-Malayin, 6th impression

Principal references in English

BOULANGER, Pierre-Marie (2008), Sustainable Development Indicators: a scientific challenge, a democratic issue. *SAPIENS* vol. 1, no. 1. Website: http://sapiens.revues.org/166

DEUTSCHE WELLE (2008), Africa's Plight Dominates First day of G8 Summit. DW website:http://www.dw.de/dw/article/ 0,,3466618,00.html

GJELTEN, Tom (2009), Economic Crisis Poses Threat to Global Stability. 18 February 2009. NPR website: http://www.npr.org/templates/story/ story.php?storyId=100781975

HALLIDAY, Fred (2000), Global Governance: Prospects and Problems. *Citizenship Studies*, vol. 4, no. 1, February 2000, 19–33

HASNA, Abdallah M. (2007), Dimensions of Sustainability. *Journal of Engineering for Sustainable Development*, 2 (1), 47–57

INTERNATIONAL INSTITUTE FOR SUSTAINABLE DEVELOPMENT, What is Sustainable Development? Website: http://www.iisd.org/sd/

INTERNATIONAL SOCIAL SCIENCE JOURNAL, Governance, vol. 50, issue 155, March 1998, p. 157

NORGAARD, Richard B. (1994), *Development Betrayed: the End of Progress and a Co-evolutionary Revisioning of the Future.* London and New York : Routledge Chapman Hall

PADDY, Allen (2009), Global Recession – Where did all the money go? London: *The Guardian*, 29 January

PEOPLE'S DAILY (2009), China Heads to Europe for Multi-billion Trade Deal. 25 February 2009. Website:http://english.people.com.cn/ 90001/90780/91421/6600900.html

RHODES, R. A. W. (1996), The New Governance: governing without government. *Political Studies*, vol. 44, no. 4, 652–67. Available online: http://law.hku.hk/gl/rhodes.pdf

ROUBINI, Nouriel (2009), A Global Breakdown of the Recession in 2009. Forbes.com website: http://www.forbes.com/2009/01/14/global-recession-2009-oped-cx_nr_0115roubini.html

SESSIONS, George, ed. (1995), Deep Ecology for the 21st Century: Readings on the Philosophy and Practice of the New Environmentalism. Boston: Shambala

McBRIDE, Stephen and WISEMAN, John, (eds.) (2000), *Globalisation and Its Discontents*. New York: St Martin's Press

UNITED NATIONS CONFERENCE ON TRADE AND DEVELOPMENT (2004), Development and Globalisation: Facts and Figures. New York and Geneva: UNCTAD

Index

In alphabetising, Al- and Ibn are ignored.